The High Achiever's Guide

Praise for
The High Achiever's Guide

"Maki reminds us to change the arc of our existence by setting the bar HIGHER and demanding more from life. Read this book and reclaim what you want out of your life, instead of resigning yourself to making the best out of circumstances that only meet the status quo."

—**Richie Norton**, bestselling author of *The Power of Starting Something Stupid*

"In her new and wonderfully insightful book, Maki Moussavi turns professional success upside down—sure, you may have passed many of the mileposts traditionally associated with 'success,' but by whose definition? And how does it impact your own personal happiness and fulfillment? Maki knows why many 'high achievers' still feel empty inside and provides a systematic, step-by-step approach to getting in touch with what you REALLY want out of life and work....and how to achieve THAT!"

—**Dr. Cindy McGovern**, author of *Every Job Is a Sales Job*

"If everyone around you is convinced you have it all together, but you are not so sure you do, *The High Achievers Guide* is for you. Maki Moussavi offers up her own journey toward fulfillment in a delightfully candid way. Now as a coach she has turned her discoveries into steps that others can follow."

—**Lori Michele Leavitt**, author of *The Pivot: Orchestrating Extraordinary Business Momentum*

"It's never too late to pursue your dreams. Maki Moussavi guides us to take action and commit to the vision we have for our lives. This book is an important reminder that we are all dreamers—but we have to choose to pursue the dream and take action to make those dreams a reality."

—**Robin Farmanfarmaian**, professional speaker and entrepreneur, CEO & cofounder of Applied Reality Overlays

"Maki Moussavi's latest book *The High Achiever's Guide* grabbed me right from the beginning. She bravely acknowledges her issues of feeling there should be something more. She shares that there is a dark side to what drives us; we must face our fears and overcome those voices in our heads that get in our way. She reveals a systematic approach, utilizing curiosity to uncover an exhilarating self-development process to lead you on your quest for fulfillment."

—**Dr. Diane Hamilton**, CEO of Tonerra, author of *Cracking the Curiosity Code*

"This book is perfect for anyone aiming to finally take control of their destiny. A kind kick in the pants to believe the truth about ourselves and spur us toward greatness."

—**Olga V. Mack,** VP of Strategy at Quantstamp, founder of Women Serve on Boards, and author of *Get on Board: Earning your Ticket to a Board Seat* and *Fundamentals of Smart Contract Security*

The High Achiever's Guide

Transform Your Success Mindset and Begin the Quest to Fulfillment

Maki Moussavi

wisdom tree

Cover and Layout Design: Jermaine Lau

First published in India in 2020 by agreement with Mango Publishing Group

ISBN 978-81-8328-545-2

Published by
Wisdom Tree
4779/23, Ansari Road
Darya Ganj, New Delhi-110 002
Ph.: 011-23247966/67/68
wisdomtreebooks@gmail.com

Printed in India

For my little birdies, Syra and Sansa, who give me wings, and for my husband, Payam, who sees me.

Never love anybody who treats you like you're ordinary.
—Oscar Wilde

Table of Contents

Introduction

Are you successful yet strangely empty? Is there a void you can't fill, no matter how much money you make, status you achieve, things you buy, or trips you go on? Maybe you're doing okay, but still feel as if there should be something more. Do you change things up in an attempt to find the mystery puzzle piece, only to find that the sense of a missing element returns once you've adjusted to the new normal? Do you wonder if there must be something wrong with you and worry that you'll never be satisfied? If so, you might be a high achiever.

At the height of my career, when I was finally where I'd always wanted to be, making more money than I ever had, I was miserable. It made no sense. I couldn't identify why, and as my awareness of just how unhappy I was increased, it took up more and more space in my head until it consumed me. I thought, "I'm damaged in some fundamental way. Why can't I be happy?" The irony is that, for my most of my adult life, I have focused on gratitude and appreciation for what I do have. I was grateful for my work, my home, my family, my health, my friends, even for the coffee I lingered over daily, enjoying every sip. I had clarity about all that I had going for me. Yet, somehow, it wasn't enough. I didn't know why and had no idea how to fix it.

I started tuning in to my coworkers in a different way. I realized that, though the circumstances of our lives varied, many of them felt similarly to me. They "had it all," but it didn't feel like much. They were exhausted, put upon, bored, anxious, depressed, overwhelmed, stressed out, running on fumes, irritable, frustrated—the list goes on. Oddly, it reassured me that I wasn't alone. Not in a misery-loves-company kind of way, but in a way that sparked the thought that we all shared something in common that could be identified with the right tools, if I could find them.

When I began the quest for "the answer," I was pumped up. Ready to figure it out and tackle it the way I had every other challenge in my life to that point. I did some research and decided to start by reading self-help books. There are so many options it was hard to know which would be most helpful. I scanned summaries, looked at reviews, and ultimately decided to begin with books that had a more spiritual bent, because every business-oriented book out there felt much too "corporate" and formulaic to me. I got to work.

I learned a lot. Each book had something interesting and relevant to offer that I could work with. I kept reading. Over time, I had a hodge-podge of information and no clue how to begin making real changes. I did some experimenting and found that I would make some headway, then get stuck, unsure of how to keep going or how to take what I had done to the next level. I was just so steeped in the way I thought and operated that, even if the change I tried to make made sense logically, getting my brain to think in new ways was a lot harder than I had anticipated.

Eventually, I came to the realization that what I really wanted was barely considered from day to day. I did the things that I had been taught mattered, and that were reinforced daily through habit and routine. My survival was covered. I had a home, money, family, food, and health. I was grateful for all of it. But it was *survival*. Joy, excitement, and inspiration were rare. I wasn't truly experiencing life through the lens of thriving. Neither were most of the people who surrounded me.

This is how high achievers come to a place of stagnation and lack of fulfillment. Your bar is *too freaking low*. You live in the place of low expectations, where survival is good enough. You rarely tip the balance into truly experiencing your life more often than not. You grind it out. You learned from those who came before you and those who surround you that you should be grateful for what you have and make the best of it. To want more is unrealistic and perhaps even silly. After all, this is what your parents did and what your friends do now. Suck it up, buttercup. Maybe buy an expensive toy or take an extravagant trip to fill the void. Deal with it and settle in. This is your life.

"I'll be okay," "It will be fine," "I'm alright"—do you say things like this to yourself on a regular basis? Okay, fine, alright. These are words of resignation. If you reinforce through your words and thoughts that all you expect is to be okay, then okay is all you'll be. We live in a world of imbalance, where we see those who have less than we do and feel guilty or shameful for wanting more than we already have. How does your shame or guilt help those who have less than you? Raise your bar, begin demanding more from life, get out of your own misery, and then you can actually dedicate time, energy, and/or money to helping those less fortunate than you.

As a high achiever, you are beautifully equipped to lead a fulfilled life. But first, you have to acknowledge that what drives you may be a bit dark. The need to be validated, acknowledged, accomplished, seen, recognized, to win, etc., are drivers that come from a place of limited self-worth. You may be thinking, "Wait a minute. I'm self-confident. I know what I'm worth." But do you really? Your self-confidence is bolstered by the validation you receive for meeting the expectations of others. Would your confidence remain intact if you didn't receive recognition? You don't know your value internally, so you seek to have it defined externally. As you know, these drivers will work for a while. You'll enter the achieve/receive validation cycle and it will feed itself, all while you remain void of the knowledge of your intrinsic worth. You will make money, achieve status, accumulate material possessions, and remain unfulfilled. The tangible cannot fill the intangible hole inside of you.

As successful as you are, you can't take your life to the next level without doing the deep work to transform the way you see yourself and raise the bar for what you expect from life. The way you live has been dictated from the outside with little to no input from you. How can you possibly expect fulfillment if what *you* want isn't at the heart of all you do? Yes, it will be scary. You must have the courage to walk out of step with those who surround you. You must have the conviction that it's worth facing the fear to live a life in which you can thrive rather than survive. Neither the courage nor the conviction will show up to support you as long as your desires remain unconsidered. This is YOUR life. Not your mom's, dad's, kid's, partner's, or friend's. Yours.

There is no right time to do this work. It will never be convenient. It will never be easy. You don't know how much longer you'll be here. Even if you live to be 102, don't you want to live with high expectations and experiences to match for as many days as you possibly can? Don't you want to role-model that way of living to those who surround you? Change is not made by those who fall in line. It's made by those who go against the grain and challenge the status quo. The sooner you demand more and step up to make it happen, the faster you'll reap the rewards and benefits of having done so.

I am you. I've been where you are. I made a commitment to myself to do it differently. I've done everything I lay out in this guide and am still doing it, because the work is never really done. You will never stop growing and expanding unless you make a conscious decision and fight tooth and nail to stay stagnant. Each new level you reach comes with its own devil, but that won't even matter to you. You may even enjoy facing down the new devil because you know how to do it. This book is about how to get out of your own way. The process laid out will create a new way of operating that you can use for the rest of your life to continue expanding and finding a holistic, redefined kind of success that has eluded you thus far.

If you're a high achiever who:

- "Has it all" but remains unfulfilled
- Feels there must be more to life
- Has success but struggles with overwhelm, stress, anxiety, etc.
- Is settling for okay when you really want more
- Wants to have a higher purpose

then it's time to transform your success mindset and get on the path that will take you to where you really want to be. In *The High Achiever's Guide,* you'll learn how to do this by examining how you got here, what drives you, how you hold yourself back, and what it takes to define your new vision for life by facing fear, using your voice, trusting your instincts, and committing to a new way of being.

You are here for a reason. Your life is not about grinding it out to merely settle for less. You're a high achiever. You're built for this transformation. Are you ready?

PART I

Congratulations, You're a Computer

CHAPTER 1

You've Been Programmed

How did I get here?

The question nagged at me. It would pop into my head in the chaos of trying to get out the door in the morning when I was going to be late again, dammit. It made another appearance when I pulled into the parking lot, anxious about what the day would bring. The question would pop up over and over again, while under the glare of the fluorescent lights, reading the emails that signaled the day's fire drills, wanting to slide right out of my chair into a pile under my desk. I couldn't follow through on answering this question. I would begin to ponder it, the depressing evidence of how I had created my reality would pile up, and I knew that I had somehow, unintentionally, been the architect of my own despair. I tried to move on from it, but then this question's best friend asked:

What do you want?

This was it. The million-dollar question. The one I didn't know how to answer. I didn't even know where to start and, up to that point, there had been precious few times in my life when I wasn't sure how to start and couldn't come up with *something* that would get me on the path. How was it possible to not know what I wanted? Was I the only one whose internal response was the equivalent of an exasperated shrug? It made me oddly uncomfortable, as if there must have been something missing from me to not have a response to such a fundamental question.

I became obsessed with finding the answer. As I started to dig through my own mental clutter, it started to make perfect sense that what I wanted wasn't immediately obvious. In our fast-paced world, we barely take a breath between one activity and the next. Our poor brains are inundated with constant stimulation. We are listening, reading, scrolling, participating, going, traveling, worrying, analyzing, thinking, and, well, basically just doing entirely too much shit. Worse yet, we are so used to doing entirely too much that we don't know how *not* to do it. It shouldn't come as any surprise that we have severely diminished capacity for tapping into our truest selves. We can't hear anything above the continuous noise that we've come to accept as integral to our daily lives.

When this journey started, I was completely immersed in the cycle of "busy-ness." I moved constantly. Relaxation was a foreign concept. When I wasn't at work, I bustled around, tidying up, making dinner, getting the kids what they needed, remembering that thing I needed to do, responding to an email, watching the clock to make sure I got my workout in before midnight, fretting about how I was going to get enough sleep when I had so much left to do and was already behind on rest—an endless litany of thoughts piled up on top of one another, increasing my anxiety as the day went on. If nothing needed to be done, I would stand there and look around, trying to identify something that could use attention. WTF.

It was like an addiction, this need to "accomplish." It made me a bit of a crazy person. My husband didn't suffer from this affliction. I would get so mad at him for just sitting. How could he sit on that couch, chill out, and watch a show when there was so much to do, for God's sake? Don't get me wrong—my husband is pretty amazing. He's truly my partner in every way, but one thing he had down that I was failing at miserably was the ability to just *be*. To sit and do nothing for just a little while. To shut it down, the whole messy monkey circus in my head that was in a constant poo-throwing frenzy. Honestly, I was jealous of his ability to turn it all off for a little while. I couldn't do it.

All the mental and physical doing that I was continuously engaged in settled into my body in the form of symptoms like tightness in my chest, insomnia, and irritability. That last one, though. Everything got on my nerves. I woke up in a state of irritation and it was all downhill from there. It was actually this consistent state of irritation that served as the pivotal wake-up call for me. It was the car alarm that kept going off, until I finally reached the point where that sucker needed to be silenced. I couldn't persist in that state. I didn't like what it was doing to the way I related to my children. It seemed like I was always snapping at them for doing kid things, like wandering around in the morning with no sense of urgency. Didn't they know I had a meeting to get to, for Pete's sweet sake? Of course, I never said these things aloud, but I wasn't proud of my impatience. It made me sad to think that my daily interactions with my kids were always rushed. We rushed out the door in the morning, rushed home to make sure dinner, homework, bath time, and bedtime all happened in a timely manner. If work needed to be done, it got squeezed in after all of that, and the only time I had for workouts was late at night. More often than not I'd be finishing up a workout at ten thirty at night, just in time to collapse into bed and start over again after six hours of sleep, if that.

How did I let my life get this way? And I wasn't the only one. How did the collective "we," the high achievers, get this way?

It all comes down to programming: the accumulation of the experiences that shapes our lives, that limits how we see ourselves, and that, along with continuous exposure to the expectations of the outside world, drowns out who we are at the core of our beings. The barrage of outside information invades our minds, takes up residence, and creates such a cacophony that, even though something is wrong, all we have to go on is this vague sense of unease that we cannot name or describe; we are so out of touch with who we are elementally.

There is no easy button for addressing how we came to be this way. We are like computers without the benefit of system updates to clear out the outdated crap and bugs in the system that no longer serve us. It is absolutely essential to clear the antiquated programming and to replace it with a sleek and self-efficacious operating system, one that does away with the old and busted to make way for the new hotness.

It's overwhelming at first. How to begin? In this guide, you will be presented with a systematic approach that breaks down the process into manageable chunks that you can do a bit at a time. If there is one key thought to keep in your mind throughout what we will cover in this book, it's this: You do not need to have the answers. Come with curiosity and compassion toward yourself, suspend judgment, and observe. Answer the questions at hand and the more complex answers will take shape and appear when it's time, when you are capable of accepting them because of your progress on this self-development journey. It took you years and years to become how you are today. All those experiences came together to make you the high achiever you are. You will not undo it overnight, and trust me, you would miss all the fun if you could! You may be scoffing to yourself now, thinking "Yeah, right! Fun? This chick is crazy." It's okay that you don't believe me yet. But the sense of empowerment and the clarity you will create if you follow the process are not only fun, but downright exhilarating. You are worthy of investing this effort in yourself. Make the decision, right here and now, that your life is worth this investment of time and energy, and remind yourself of that as often as needed. When it gets tough, recommit. We will talk much more about how to keep going when you're losing steam a little later. For now, this first commitment to yourself is the most powerful move you can make to change your life.

Now that you're in it to win it, it's time to get into the external influences that have shaped the way you operate today. There are many, many sources of programming, so for the sake of simplicity, let's focus on the following categories. Keep in mind that each of these is highly complex and loaded with lots of considerations. The list of questions for each is meant to get your self-examination juices flowing. It's important to get your head into the right space for looking at your programming. Starting with a limited list will trigger the process, and it will naturally continue once you've started.

Sources of Programming

Family relationships. Consider your relationship with your parents, their marital status, how old they were when they had you, whether they had close parental or family relationships, your sibling relationships, whether you had grandparents or extended family in your life, the dynamics of your family, expectations for behavior, what made a good son or daughter, what you were or weren't allowed to talk about, and so on.

Socioeconomic status. How much money did your family have? Were finances a source of anxiety? What kind of home did you grow up in, and what part of town was it in? Did you get to wear what you wanted, or were you stuck with hand-me-downs? Did your status make you a target for teasing or ridicule? Did you have so much it made you uncomfortable, like you were flashing your wealth in the faces of those who didn't have as much? What about the kids you hung out with? Did you stick with those who had similar backgrounds? What labels did your family/friends use for those who had more or less than you did?

Cultural background. Are you part of an immigrant or ethnic minority? How did it influence the way you were raised? Was your life a blend of that culture and the one you were raised in? What are the expectations and value system of your culture of origin? What challenges came with this experience? Did you feel those outside your experience didn't understand your family or its priorities? What slurs or comments did you hear that targeted your ethnic group?

Geographic location. Did you grow up in a rural or urban area? What are the values and norms of the area? Is there a particular identity associated with that region? Is it agricultural, industrial, coastal, etc.? How did your location influence your thoughts about what a "normal" childhood experience should look like? How do the values of that upbringing show up in your life today? Did you long to escape the kind of environment you grew up in? Did you decide early on it was the only way of life for you and stay put? Why did you want to leave or stay?

Political and religious influences. Was religion important when you were growing up? What beliefs did your religious upbringing ingrain within you? What are the politics of your family or the part of the world you grew up in? Is or was there any conflict between your religious and political belief systems? Are your current beliefs in line or at odds with how or where you were raised? How do you think about those whose belief systems don't align with yours?

Social network. Who are your friends? Who do you spend time with? How do all of the above factors influence your chosen network? Has that changed over the course of your life, or has it remained consistent? Do you seek out those who are like-minded, different from you, or some of both? Do you find yourself trying to stay in line with the expectations of your group? Do you silence yourself to fit in? How does this network uplift you or bring you down?

Remember that you don't have to know the answers to all of these questions just yet, but seeing the various angles in black and white should instill an appreciation for just how complex our programming truly is. When I started to do this work on myself, I realized how little awareness I'd had around the experiences that had formed me. They were just my experiences; I hadn't ascribed any particular meaning or weight to them. One of the benefits of this exercise is that it gives you the opportunity to think about who you are through a layered approach that will hopefully show you how awesome you are to have come through what you have.

If you're tempted to dismiss the exercise because your life was "easy" and privileged, don't. Our programming in and of itself isn't good or bad—it just is. Its *impact* on you is the real point of digging into it. You're reading these words because you believe your life can be better. Remain open and don't close the door on any element of examination based on preconceived notions.

My own programming played a huge role in where I was when I began this process. For me, the question "What do you want?" couldn't effectively be answered until I understood why I was so far removed from where I wanted to be in the first place. I had to look at the influences and expectations that had shaped my life, and that was no straightforward task. As the child of immigrants, my early life included a hodge-podge of influences. We lived in student housing; my parents were closely tied in with their cultural group but also had many American friends. We didn't have much money, but I always received the best educationally because we lived in a college town where the learning standards were high. My own parents came from a culture that valued higher education, so I learned early on that being a good student and eventually going to college and beyond was the righteous path. We had very little extended family around. I only ever met one of my grandparents and didn't really get to know her because the visits were brief. Naturally, most of my friends were in the same lower-middle-class bracket, which made it easy for us to understand one another and relate to each other's experiences, especially in elementary school.

As our world became larger in middle and high school, the influencing factors and the lens through which we viewed the world began to shift. There was a whole other place outside the little neighborhood where we could walk to one another's front doors, school, or the pool in the summer. We experienced everything within a mile of where we slept until it was time to get on the bus for middle school, where we finally met and interacted with kids from all over town, no longer limited to our little bubble. But even as those influences within our microcosm grew, some things remained constant. We grew up in an agricultural state in a college town, surrounded by rural farmland. A border state that was on the side of the north in the Civil War, there were vast differences in culture between our state and the one next door that we would sometimes drive to for camping excursions. There were and are a lot of misconceptions about my state, Kansas, and to this day, when people ask where I'm from and I answer "Manhattan," they assume

I'm talking about New York. It blows their minds that someone like me could have grown up in a small town in Kansas, and it's even more confusing to many how on earth my parents ended up there as immigrants from Iran, of all places. I grew up without religion; my parents were open to letting me attend church with my friends if I asked, but there was no particular reinforcement of any one belief system. Politically, they were liberal and highly engaged in politics, as they and their families had been greatly impacted by the internal and global politics that shaped the conflict and regime change in Iran.

My early experiences formed the backdrop and led to the formation of the limiting beliefs that came to shape my standard mode of operation. Limiting beliefs are the thoughts that keep you from moving forward by diminishing your belief in yourself and what you're capable of. There are a couple of lenses through which limiting beliefs affect you. The first lens is that through which you view yourself and whether your capabilities are enough. The second lens is that through which you view the world and how you see its limitations, and what impact those limitations have on your own life.

The following represent common limiting beliefs with regard to the self:

- I can't pull that off.
- This is all I know.
- I'll never be able to [fill in the blank].
- I never say the right thing.
- This always happens to me.
- I don't have what it takes.
- I didn't finish school, so I'm not smart enough to [fill in the blank].

Add these up, and what you end up with is "**I am not enough.**"

This next list details some thoughts that represent limiting beliefs with respect to the external world:

- The world is a terrible place.
- It's scary to go out in public not knowing what may happen.
- The rich get richer and the poor get poorer.
- It's all falling apart, and it gets worse every day.
- There's not enough [fill in the blank] to go around.

The general theme with limiting beliefs regarding the external world is "**There is not enough,**" whether it be enough money, food, compassion, sense, etc. It paints a picture of an unfriendly place, one that is against you, so what's the point of trying anyway? In the extreme, thoughts like this can lead to defeatism, in which you being the loser is a foregone conclusion, or extremism, in which you view yourself as a lone crusader, constantly fighting and thrashing against the status quo. A healthy balance between practicality and optimism is the best way to move forward, and we'll talk more about that later in the book.

My personal limiting beliefs were not completely unknown to me, but going through the exercise of contemplating and writing them down was eye-opening. I'd been walking around with some serious BS in my head about what I was capable of and what options were open to me. Here is a sampling of my own limiting beliefs that may help as you begin considering your own:

- This is all I know. I'm limited to this field.
- I don't have what it takes to work for myself.
- People will see through me.
- No one wants what I have to offer.
- If I don't have status, I'll become insignificant.
- I can't make the kind of money I want if I leave.

I could go on, but you get the gist. These are all of the "I am not enough" variety. When I dug into these beliefs and really thought about them, I realized how strangely basic they were: egocentric and concerned with being small, unseen, and unheard. Thoughts of this nature had been such an integral part of my thinking, embedded in my mind as if they were factual, that I didn't have any reason to take a hard look at them and see them for the weirdly insignificant thoughts they were. You will have the same realizations, and you will be freed from the limiting beliefs that bind you if you have the courage to face them head-on. After going through the identification process, my response to my own beliefs was some variation of "That's dumb!" or "So what?" or "That's not even true." People don't like the real me? So what? I don't have what it takes? That's not even true. I don't know enough to work in a different field? That's dumb. And not true. Think of what you'd say to a friend who was confessing their own limiting beliefs to you. How would you respond? Chances are, it would not be with "You're right. You totally suck. That will never work. Don't even try." We are much more generous and compassionate when talking with others. Act as your own friend when you become aware of your limiting beliefs, and defuse their power over you.

Because you've been programmed, the key to unlocking your transformation is to rewrite the programming and patterns that are keeping you in the hamster wheel of stagnation. As a high achiever, you have within you everything you need to do just that, but it can be hard to make the leap from a whole lot of what's not working to what will actually serve you instead. I also know that, as a high achiever, you likely love your checklists and goals, so for that reason, in each chapter, I'm going to share a brief "To Don't" list that you can use to keep yourself on track throughout the process.

To Don't:

- **Don't judge yourself** as you dig into your programming. We each have our own to deal with.
- **Don't try to fast-forward through the process**. It will take time to undo years of unconscious beliefs.
- **Don't let your limited view of yourself stop you** in your tracks. There's a more powerful version of you beneath that limited view that you are trying to reach.

Do Instead:

- **Remember that your experiences have shaped who you are today**. You wouldn't be the kickass high achiever you are without them.
- **Stay curious and compassionate.** Treat yourself as you would a dear friend.
- **Invest the time and energy** it takes to get started. You only need a few minutes of focused time each day.

Summing Up

Your personal sources of programming provide critical insight into how you got to where you are today. In our quick-fix way of life, it can be tempting to fast-forward to the remedy, but there's no way around doing the deep work. Roll up your sleeves and get to it. The understanding you will gain about yourself and others as you do this work is priceless. You will walk away with a newfound appreciation of who you are and how you came to be, beginning to chip away at the self-doubt that keeps you from moving forward. I encourage you to keep a journal as you work your way through the process. There's no better way to pleasantly surprise yourself than to look back and see how far you've come.

Remember:

- You've been programmed by many influences at work in your life, including your family dynamics, socioeconomic status, geographic location, political and religious influences, social network, etc.
- Limiting beliefs are formed through our experiences and sources of programming. There are two basic lenses through which we see limitations: the lens through which we view ourselves and the lens through which we view the world.
- Up to this point, you have been heavily influenced by the external world and its expectations, which naturally leads to stagnation as you are not expressing who you truly are, rather marching to the drumbeat that many others are marching to in the absence of a personal definition of success.
- Understanding your personal programming lays the foundation for going from a lack of fulfillment to empowered self-expression and intentional creation.

Get out your journal or laptop and begin your self-examination by contemplating the following questions.

1. Create a table or list and write down the thoughts that come to mind for each of these categories: family dynamics, socioeconomic status, geographic location, political and

religious influences, social relationships, and whatever else comes to mind for you. Think in terms of the influence of each of these on you from early life until now. If one of these categories is particularly significant for you, spend some additional time focusing on just that area. For instance, if your family was active in the church and you suffered abuse at the hands of someone respected, how did what you were taught influence the way you decided how to handle the situation? Remember, do not judge yourself. Programming is incredibly powerful. Nothing you did or didn't do is reason to be down on yourself. It just is, and now is the time to understand why.

2. Start identifying your limiting beliefs. When you consider doing something new or out of the ordinary, what thoughts pop into your head? If it helps, review the list earlier in the chapter until you get rolling. You can separate these into beliefs about yourself versus beliefs about the world around you, if that helps with focus.
3. Once you have some of your limiting beliefs down on paper, ask yourself the following about each:

    a. Are they your words or someone else's? Have those words been spoken before, about you or around you?
    b. Do they contain absolutes, like always or never? Those words should be automatic triggers to identifying that particular belief as untrue.
    c. Do they point fingers or look externally rather than internally? For instance, a thought like "They always gang up on me" looks outward to blame instead of inwardly asking "Why am I tolerating this?"
    d. Are they excuses? Are you saying to yourself "I don't have time" to do what should be high on your priority list? Again, the point is not to judge yourself, but to see where you are participating in holding yourself back.

As you keep track of your thoughts throughout this process, remember to date your entries and to keep your journal handy. If you have an important realization when you're out and about, you can use the voice memo app on your phone to quickly record your thoughts and review them later when you have time to sit down and listen. Even if you've never journaled before in your life, now is the time to begin. Writing or otherwise communicating what's happening in the analytical part of your brain helps get the other side of your brain engaged in processing, which will lead to breakthroughs for you as you continue through the process.

CHAPTER 2

Toxic Fumes

Now that we've established how good high achievers are at meeting the expectations of the world around them, it's time to talk about the most damaging set of expectations you will ever be subjected to—those imposed upon you by participating in toxic relationships. You may be wondering why we need to talk about your relationships in the context of transforming your success mindset. It's simple, really; try as you might, it's impossible to compartmentalize your work life and your personal life. When something is amiss in one aspect of your life, it shows up in the other, whether you recognize it or not. As a high achiever, you're accustomed to endurance, bearing pain and discomfort even when it doesn't serve you. Interpersonal programming is just as critical to growth in all aspects of your life as all the external sources of programming we just covered. It's easy to dismiss what's happening in our relationships with others in our lives when we are focused on a single area like work. However, when toxicity is present, it is pervasive, infecting every aspect of how we think and operate.

Toxicity can be obvious, but it can also fly under the radar, impacting you in a vague and disquieting way that you have a hard time articulating. You may be tempted to dismiss it because it's hard to justify how you feel to others, or you may have a sense of shame for being in a toxic situation that you feel powerless to change.

Whether you can put it into words or not, it's having a profoundly negative impact on your life that must be addressed ASAP.

The interactions and experiences we have with those who have little to no regard for the people around them can cause us tremendous pain that inflicts long-lasting damage. It's like a poison that you continue to breathe in as long as you tolerate interactions with people who do this to you. We may convince ourselves there is no other choice. What if the person poisoning your atmosphere is your boss, spouse, parent, friend, or child? The proximity of the relationship can lead to a sense of defeat before you've begun. How is it possible to change the dynamic that you've participated in so fully when you know the reaction of the person in question is what you want to avoid at all costs?

Not only is it possible, it's absolutely necessary. No matter how much you accomplish in every single aspect of personal development, if you do not clean up the toxic leaks in your life, you will not make it as far as you want to go. Toxicity is the ultimate mind poison. It ruins your peace of mind, puts you on edge, makes you feel cornered, and steals any chance you have at joy. Worst of all, you participate in your own destruction when you allow it to go on unchecked.

If you are thinking, "I don't have any toxic relationships in my life—I can skip this chapter!" you either a) are the luckiest son-of-a-gun ever or b) haven't registered subtle behaviors as toxic. The easiest way to identify subtle toxicity is by considering your own emotional state. Look at the following list and determine whether you feel any of these in your current relationships: drained, depleted, cautious, avoidant, on edge, nervous, anxious, guilty, tense, etc. Interactions that arouse these feelings are highly likely to have a toxic component that you haven't yet recognized. Pay special attention to your family relationships! Do not assume that everyone's mother makes them feel the way yours does. When you grow up in dysfunction, it's such an inherent part of your life that it normalizes your experiences and makes it harder to see that which signals a problem.

Do not confuse toxicity with intention to harm. Toxicity is a mode of operation, a second-nature way of interacting with others that is not necessarily completely conscious. It's ingrained. It's how toxic people relate. If your recognition of toxicity is limited to the narcissistic/sociopathic end of the spectrum, it's time to expand your understanding so you can identify red-flag behaviors when they present themselves. Keep in mind that toxic behavior does not come in a physically obvious package. Toxic people don't necessarily look or behave like monsters. They can be charming, sociable, respected, and so on. Toxicity that comes in a pretty package can be very confusing to those they interact with. Their presentation makes it harder to justify the perception of toxicity, even to yourself. Do not dismiss toxicity because of the proximity of the relationship or how someone is generally perceived. At all times, you must honor how you feel in interaction with these people above logic and appearances. Your feelings are valid. Trust yourself.

In our world today, there is a lot of overtly toxic behavior that is easy to identify, steer clear of, or speak up against. However, not all toxicity is obvious; subtly poisonous behavior can be far more dangerous. It's harder to identify, can make you question your sanity or perception of reality, and can cause you to discount your intuition when it tells you that something is wrong because it's hard to "prove" it.

Signs and Symptoms of Toxic Behavior

Keep front and center this fundamental truth about toxicity:

The toxic person is a manipulator.

Remember at all times that the point of toxic interactions is to manipulate you. The manipulator feels entitled to whatever it is you have that they need, whether that is your patience, compassion, time, connections, etc. They take without giving. In the context of mutual respect, reciprocity is a healthy component of connecting with others. You give generously to those you respect, freely and without expectation of receiving something in return. Even though you don't expect it, those you give to return your generosity in other ways over the course of time. There is an ocean of difference between normal, healthy interactions and those where the manipulator seeks to take, take, take and feels entitled to take even more if you'll allow them to. Toxic people are energy vampires who suck up your life force and leave you feeling depleted rather than energized. They may create a sense of urgency, display exaggerated reactions to any kind of questioning or confrontation, and generally expect that you fall in line with whatever it is they demand of you. You find yourself doing the dance and giving in time and time again to avoid the consequences of not meeting their demands. And that, my friend, is how they train you to stay in the cycle of dysfunction.

At the heart of all toxic relationships is a **lack of boundaries.** Those who want to manipulate you don't see you as a wholly separate entity with free will. They see you as someone who exists to meet their needs, and if manipulation is required to make that happen, they roll up their sleeves and get to work. The challenge is that those who employ manipulation against you are often those who are closest to you. Not only may they be your family members, but also friends, coworkers, and/or even your partner. It can be challenging to navigate such interactions when you know any discussion of how their behavior makes you feel could end in a ridiculous display of emotion that you'd rather not deal with. It could be that you've tried to talk to this person before and it had no impact at all. You may turn to using logic on yourself in an attempt to overcome your unsettling feelings, which, in case you haven't noticed, doesn't work. It's like using a gun to kill smoke. Knowing the signs and symptoms of toxic behavior will help you identify whether you're involved in a toxic relationship, personally or professionally. Once you are aware of the issues, you will be armed with the knowledge required to change or leave the dynamics you are engaged in.

Manipulation Tactics

When I speak on the topic of toxicity, it frequently elicits discomfort from the audience. No one wants to believe the worst about their loved ones and friends. It's hard to wrap your mind around the fact that someone close to you may be manipulating you. To further complicate matters, the manipulator may come across as a perfectly lovely person to others, creating confusion that makes it more difficult for you to accept or explain your discomfort. Subtly manipulative behavior can be hard to discern. FOG, an acronym coined by psychologist Susan Forward, describes the emotions the manipulator uses to influence others:

F—Fear
O—Obligation
G—Guilt

In Forward's book *Emotional Blackmail* (New York: HarperCollins, 1997), she describes how manipulators use tactics that elicit these emotions to bend you to their will. They make sure you fear the consequences of crossing them, feel obligated to give them what they want out of a sense of duty, and feel guilty if you don't comply. The underlying gross factor is that you end up complicit in this dynamic by giving the manipulator what they seeks to take from you. FOG is the shit show trifecta that you will find in any manipulative scenario if you take the time to examine the dynamics at play in the relationships you suspect fall into this category.

Forward goes on to describe the types of manipulators and how each shows up with their own version of FOG.

The Punisher: Seeks a one-sided balance of power and will override you and your desires.

The Self-Punisher: If they don't get what they want, they will be upset and threaten to mess up their own lives.

The Sufferer: If you don't give in to what they want, their subsequent suffering is your fault.

The Tantalizer: Make it clear that you will get the prize they offer if you do what they demand.

In each of these archetypes, control is the ultimate goal. The manipulator doesn't care if the way they gain control is through threat or reward. Here are examples of how each of these operates in the context of the archetypes.

Punisher: Skip the happy hour with your friends or I will hurt you.

Self-punisher: Skip the happy hour with your friends or I will hurt myself.

Sufferer: Skip the happy hour with your friends. I'm so hurt that I wasn't invited. If you go, it will be your fault that I'm upset and unhappy.

Tantalizer: Skip the happy hour with your friends and I'll take you to a fancy dinner instead. They're not good enough for you, anyway.

The reason the person is manipulating you may or may not feel significant to you. What the manipulator demands isn't the point; the way in which they demand it is. By giving in to demands large and small, you establish a pattern in which the manipulator continues to use FOG to get their way, and over time their demands may escalate from the insignificant to the highly consequential. This is one slippery slope you want to stay far away from.

At times, obligation may be used in ways that don't quite add up to toxicity but are designed to take advantage of you. A friend may appeal to your sense of duty when they ask you to do something that may be inconvenient for you. They know that, because you are a "good friend," you may feel obligated to do their bidding. Is there a person in your life who consistently asks for favors? The person who thinks it's your job to take them to the airport because they don't want to pay for a ride? Or maybe it's letting their dog out three times a day for five days while they go on vacation. How can you say no when you live nearby and this person is your friend? Do you ask people for things like this? Sure, maybe sometimes. But not all the time. You can park your car at the airport, catch an Uber, board the dog, or pay a neighborhood kid to help you out. When someone in your life consistently comes to you to make their life easier, pay attention to where else in your relationship elements of manipulation are showing up. When people expect you to do whatever is easiest for them with no consideration for what that means for you, you are in an exchange where you've been taught to obey the sense of obligation rather than honoring what you really want to say or do. The person asking you knows this and uses it against you to achieve their own ends.

Another way that toxic people engage you in the cycle of manipulation is referred to as gaslighting.

> **Gaslighting:** a form of psychological manipulation that seeks to sow seeds of doubt in a targeted individual or group, making them question their own memory, perception, and sanity.

The term originated from the 1944 film *Gaslight*, in which a husband makes his wife believe she has lost her sanity because only she can see the flickering of the gaslights, when in fact he is the one causing the flickering while denying he can see what she sees. Gaslighters deny, lie, project, confuse, and ultimately wear you down in their pursuit of manipulation
(Sarkis, Stephanie. "11 Warning Signs of Gaslighting." Psychology Today. www.psychologytoday.com/us/blog/here-there-and-everywhere/201701/11-warning-signs-gaslighting).

Gaslighting can be exhausting for the person on the receiving end. To be told repeatedly that what you have seen or heard didn't happen, happened another way, or that your perception of what happened is invalid wears on you, making you question yourself rather than stand firmly in your conviction that you do, indeed, know what you experienced. Gaslighters deny and lie regarding circumstances significant and mundane; the specific subject is of no consequence. It can be tempting to dismiss denials regarding matters that don't have dire meaning or consequences—but this is precisely when you should be questioning the motive behind the denials. Why deny when not much is at stake and it would be easier in the long run to tell the truth? The allure of logic is strong, but you cannot employ it to understand the operating mode of one who manipulates. It is not logical! It is meant to impact you from an emotional perspective, and emotions aren't governed by logic. You can't explain it. Don't insist on understanding why; instead, accept what this person has shown you about who they are.

In addition to the use of FOG and gaslighting, there are several other common behaviors typical of toxic interactions that may be overt or covert.

- Non-apologies. Beware the person who cannot express true regret. Statements like "I apologize," "I'm sorry you feel that way," and "I'm sorry, but—" are not true apologies. A real apology sounds sincere and more like, "I'm sorry I hurt you. It wasn't my intention and I will be more aware of my words and actions next time."
- Refusal to accept responsibility. Toxic people are never wrong, which is why they can't truly apologize. Look for blame-shifting and victim mindset, where they either look to have someone else take the fall or turn themselves into the wronged party in any given situation.
- Controlling behavior. This may be the single most obvious way that toxicity shows up in intimate relationships. Controllers expect you to comply with their rules. Their insecurity demands that they know where you are, what you're doing, whom you hang out with, why you're going, and ultimately decide whether or not you have permission to do what you wish to, based on whether they perceive a threat to their position in the who/what/were/why in question.
- Projection. People with toxic tendencies tend to project their own shortcomings by attributing them to others. For example, someone who talks down to people may accuse others of being condescending. Like the refusal to accept responsibility, it seeks to shift blame outward and away from the manipulator.
- Lack of empathy. The experience of the toxic person is paramount. No one else has suffered as much as they have; therefore, they don't have compassion for others. This can show up as competing for pain: where you might say "I was so sick last weekend," they will one-up you with stories of their own terrible illness and how they suffered more than you did. Basically, they must be the most *anything* so you get no compassion for what you've experienced.
- Lack of interest in you personally. You can engage in long one-sided conversations in which the toxic person talks incessantly about themselves and may not even remember

to ask you how you're doing. If they do remember, you may notice they don't really listen, or they jump right back into what they want to talk about instead of what's going on with you. Your feelings may be hurt that you recently told them about a significant challenge in your life and they don't remember. Your world is of limited to no significance.

- Passive aggression. Beware the quiet ones. Just because someone is soft-spoken doesn't mean they can't be toxic. The passive-aggressive types get away with more toxic behavior because they're not as loud, but do not mistake quiet for non-toxic. These are the people who may be nice to you in person while talking about you behind your back, make underhanded cutting remarks and then feign innocence when called out, employ a lot of facial expressions to disrupt but won't use their words, etc. Passive aggression is particularly difficult to verbalize because, by design, it's not as obvious and therefore it's easier to deny the motive behind the behavior.

If you are dealing with a particularly malignant toxicity that seems to check every box we've discussed so far, you may be dealing with someone who has a personality disorder. The information shared here is not meant to be diagnostic; if you suspect an underlying disorder, contact a therapist or do some research, being careful to stick with reputable sources of information. Cluster B personality disorders as described in the Diagnostic and Statistical Manual of Mental Disorders are characterized by dramatic, overly emotional, or unpredictable thinking and behavior. The personality disorders included in Cluster B are antisocial, borderline, histrionic, and narcissistic, and many of these personality types include the kinds of behaviors summarized here. If you are in fact dealing with someone who has a personality disorder, there are specific recommendations for how to engage with them and protect yourself that a therapist or professional can help you with.

Workplace Toxicity

In my corporate life, there were epic levels of toxicity all around me. Consistently floored by the ridiculous behavior, I couldn't understand why such noxious behavior was tolerated. Toxic behaviors were perpetrated by those who were "nice" and could be charming, while others didn't bother to mask their dysfunction. Either way, they employed the tactics that worked for them specifically, with no incentive to change because they were getting away with the bad behavior. Here are some archetypes to illustrate the kinds of coworker or leader to be on alert for:

- **The martyr** is nice and accommodating on the surface but highly passive-aggressive. He may not vocalize his thoughts and opinions, but will make faces in meetings, try to recruit the support of others to his "side" when in disagreement with someone, behave as if he respects you but then bad-mouth you to anyone who will listen. When confronted about his behavior, he may act shocked, cry, deny, and shift blame to others for their actions. The martyr lowers team morale by expecting others to operate at his level or accommodate his weaknesses with no consideration for how it impacts others to do so.
- **The egomaniac** is self-centered, with an enormous sense of entitlement. She may feel like some "star" quality she possesses makes her indispensable, and as such expects any bad behavior on her part to be overlooked in favor of keeping her happy and productive. This type may not bother to be pleasing; she expects others to please her. She demands accolades and special treatment and is quick to point fingers at others when called out about her behavior.
- **The tyrant** is the egomaniac hopped up on the power of authority. Bad behavior, including overly dramatic reactions, outbursts, insults, inappropriate relationships, etc., are all potentially part of the package that this type delivers. The same sense of entitlement that drives the egomaniac is made worse by the tyrant's ability to use it against those he sees as tools to be used for his own benefit, regardless of the impact

> on those he uses them against. The dynamics at play with the tyrant can be tricky; he was promoted despite these characteristics, which validates the bad behavior. In very unhealthy corporate cultures, he may have been promoted *because* of his character.

If you have been tolerating any of the behaviors discussed to this point, it's time to act. Not later. Now. Engaging in this dangerous pattern permeates every area of your life and undermines you in more ways than you can appreciate. It makes you an enabler, and what you enable you continue to attract. As an enabler, you are *choosing* to allow this kind of behavior. Perpetrators are highly adept at identifying targets, and they are looking specifically for people who will enable their behavior. Once you've demonstrated you'll tolerate this kind of shit, people who want to dish it out will find you to take it.

Workplace toxicity is tricky to navigate. You may feel you have limited ability to do anything about toxic behavior, depending on whether it's showing up in a coworker, direct report, or leader. The answer is not to do nothing. Talk to a trusted coworker or manager about how to approach the issue. If that's not helpful, speak to your HR representative and see if they have advice about how to handle a given situation, and begin creating a record of the behavior you observe. If you are a leader, you have an obligation to address this behavior. Don't overlook or justify it because you aren't sure what to say. Work with HR to figure out what your options are, and do what needs to be done. Enabling bad behavior in the workplace has an exponential impact that ripples throughout teams and impacts clients. Set a time to talk and have a trusted third party present, like HR, to listen or participate in the discussion. Make your expectations known and establish how you'll check in to gauge improvements in behavior. Unfortunately, it's doubtful that there are policies in place designed to address toxic behavior in the workplace. You may find that your leaders or HR department aren't particularly helpful, but you won't know until you try. If you don't get an adequate response, encourage others you trust, who also recognize the toxic behavior in question, to have their own conversations with leadership and HR. Continued feedback may be what tips the balance toward addressing the issue. If the behavior is allowed to go on unchecked, then it's time for you to consider whether you need to make a move to another department or workplace. You do have a choice in whether or not you tolerate toxic behavior.

I once assumed responsibility for a team with a couple of people who fit the martyr and egomaniac archetypes. Their behavior had gone largely unchecked for years, lowering the morale of those who had to work closely with them. The floodgates of information opened wide when I first took over the team. Those who had ongoing dealings with them had renewed hope that perhaps a new manager would take action where others hadn't. The more I learned about their behavior through my own experiences with each of them, the clearer it became just how much of an impact they had on the rest of the team. I went to my manager and HR to discuss my concerns. They were onboard with my proceeding to address the situation, so I spoke to each person directly about my expectations and began documenting our interactions. As expectations continued to go unmet, warnings were written and consequences made clear. The martyr cried and the egomaniac dismissed me as a clueless bitch who clearly didn't understand just how amazing they were. Even after extensive documentation that included the feedback of other team members, I was the one who had to eventually say, "Enough is enough. It's time to move forward to next steps." I told my manager I was done, she supported the decision, and I spoke with HR to get the wheels in motion. If I hadn't proactively sought to address the situation and eventually firmly demand an end to the cycle, nothing would have changed.

Establish Boundaries

The most effective way to handle any toxic relationship or situation is to establish boundaries. Remember that logic will not work. If you continue to try to talk with this person, expect it to be a complete waste of time and energy that takes you straight into the cycle of defensiveness, blame-shifting, and gaslighting, where nothing is accomplished and you make no progress. It's best to leave logic out of it altogether. Set the boundary, share it verbally, and make clear what the consequences are for violating that boundary. They may act confused, cry, get angry, or all of the above. You cannot control the other person's reaction, and their potential reaction should not silence you. Remain calm and respond with something that is true, but do not rationalize or justify your position.

If this sounds like a harsh approach to you, do some self-examination. Why does it feel harsh when the other person is being so clearly disrespectful of you or others, continuing to push against boundaries in an attempt to get you to back down? Setting boundaries is not a pleasant experience in the moment, because you are violating the silent terms of an agreement you have been participating in until that moment. It's uncomfortable for you because you might feel mean for doing so, and the other person's reaction is going to feed right into the fear that you are, indeed, being a meanie. Accept the discomfort as a necessary part of what must be done and do it.

Toxic people are capable of responding to boundary-setting. In order to give boundaries a real shot, you have to be incredibly vigilant about sticking to the limits you set. Be ready to enforce the consequences of a boundary violation every single time one occurs, so you can gauge whether there is any hope of a tenable long-term impact. In the professional setting, document your expectations and progress toward meeting them. In your personal life, use your best judgment to set limits, and stop wasting your effort if your boundaries aren't observed. If boundaries are observed, you may be able to maintain a relationship with this person on your own terms. The extent to which you put in effort is up to you. The manipulator may honor your boundaries for a while, then test you to see if you will let them cross the line after a period of compliance. Do not give an inch! Any flexibility on your part will be interpreted as an invitation to further push your boundaries, and you'll have to start all over again. If they continue to be noncompliant, you can begin thinking about whether you want to take a longer break and eventually cut contact with this person.

Professionally, it's important to have an established course of action for noncompliance and stick with it. In some cases, the manipulator might decide your boundaries are a deal-breaker and move on. If so, good. They've shown you it's not worth the effort to maintain a personal or professional association on someone else's terms.

For very close relationships that you wish to maintain with strict boundaries in place, the biggest favor you can do for yourself is to drop your expectations that this person will behave any differently in the future. They have shown you over and over again exactly who they are. Your choice to remain connected with boundaries that prioritize your needs is valid, but do it in a way that doesn't set you up for disappointment. Do it with compassion for yourself and the other, but with clarity that they are who they are.

I've used the term *dangerous* to describe the tolerance of toxicity in any aspect of your life, and if you continue to doubt its impact, I want to dispel that now, once and for all. Manipulators leverage the arousal of guilt and shame as a way of controlling you. Guilt and shame. Two of the most harmful emotions any of us can harbor about ourselves. They use them, deliberately, as a means to create their desired outcome. What's going on with you is the least of their concerns. When you resist, their reactions tend to be overblown in order to keep you in line, even if keeping you in line comes at the expense of your own emotional comfort. In particularly toxic relationships, where there is true malignant intent that invades multiple aspects of the relationship, the person on the receiving end of the toxicity can feel desperate to escape. If you've experienced a toxic relationship, you may have had thoughts about how life would be easier if the other person died or disappeared, triggering the guilt and shame spiral all over again. What's wrong with you that such an extreme outcome would be a relief from this endless cycle?

There is nothing wrong with you.

The fact that you feel this way is your red flag, on fire and waving in hurricane-force winds, warning you that this interaction is so poisonous you feel the only way out is for the other person to cease to exist. These emotions reveal just how terrible an impact this relationship is having on you, and how disempowered you are in this dynamic. Sometimes, the option of cutting contact with the person in question must be considered, which can trigger fear, guilt, shame, etc., about your own heartlessness. It may come to that, but there is no need to make such a heavy decision right out of the gate.

There is a caveat to all of the above. If you are in a toxic relationship with someone you are truly afraid of, do not do any of this alone. Engagement in a highly toxic relationship can create a deep sense of shame; if you haven't shared any of what you've been experiencing, it's time to confide in someone you trust. Find a therapist to work with, and if the thought of trying to establish a relationship with a new care provider is too daunting at the moment, make an appointment to see your regular doctor and let them help you. If you are in a domestic abuse situation, please seek help from The National Domestic Violence Hotline (1-800-799-SAFE) or a local support group.

As daunting as the prospect may be, establishing boundaries will be an indescribable relief to you. Once you have stopped participating in the cycle, once you act on your own behalf in a way that reflects self-respect and an empowered approach, you will feel *amazing*. It will free you, mind and soul, to remove a constant infective source of guilt, shame, and self-doubt from your life.

No discussion of toxicity is complete without addressing the impact of enabling.

> **Enabler:** a person or thing that makes something possible.

Toxicity requires the participation of the person targeted for manipulation. When you stay silent and allow the dysfunctional behavior you witness, you're a participant. If you believe it's okay because you're the only victim, two things: a) this is a glaring red flag of how little you value yourself and b) enablers are victimizers through complicity. You don't get a free pass because you aren't the toxic one, if you stand by while the manipulator does their thing. There is always collateral damage. It impacts your loved ones and, if you have children, you are setting them up to repeat the shit show you've chosen to engage in by teaching them what kind of treatment they should expect and tolerate from others. Do not lie to yourself that your children aren't aware of what's taking place. They know. If nothing else they feel it, and, when they get old enough to have their own opinions, they will be targeted with the same behavior you've been enduring. It can also impact relationships with the rest of your family, as they may have to walk on eggshells around your partner. Enabling is not a strategy. It's complicity.

To bring it all together, I'll share the story of a friend and client that showcases the cycle of toxicity in all its terrible dysfunction. Maddie is a lovely woman who is married with two children. Her parents divorced when she was a child, but her mother remarried twice, both times to abusive men. Her second marriage occurred when Maddie was in her final year of high school. Her new stepfather, Tom, had been a teacher at the high school before she was a student there. He had a reputation for inappropriate and volatile behavior, which a couple of teachers shared with Maddie under condition of anonymity. Despite Maddie's pleas that her mother delay the wedding due to this disturbing information, her mother proceeded.

Maddie moved out immediately after graduation. She'd been around Tom enough to know he was an angry, opinionated, judgmental, and volatile man. She saw him only once or twice a year and remained unaware of his contempt for her until her mother moved out for a period of time after he'd beaten her. At that point, her mother shared that for the last twenty years, he'd been referring to Maddie, her daughter, as a bitch, cunt, slut, and whore after Maddie had a relationship with a much older man.

For years, Maddie had been torn about how to handle the relationship with her mother. She treasured the closeness she shared with her sister and mother, between the toxic marriages, and found it hard to process the impact that Tom and her mother's enabling had on their relationship dynamic. Her mother expected the toxicity to unite them as fellow victims, rather than accept her role as the enabler. Her early experiences left Maddie with an inadequate sense of self-worth, which impacted her professionally. She was taught to walk on eggshells to the point that showing up confidently to her work was a challenge for her. Keeping the peace, making sure everyone else was okay and that she didn't say or do something triggering, kept her from making moves that would enhance her success. Once she recognized her perception of the toxicity was valid, she was able to establish boundaries that have freed her from the misery of participation in the cycle. She has been clear and honest with her mother and, while her mother continues to try to get her to engage in the old cycle, Maddie won't do it. She has held fast to her boundaries and feels as if a massive weight has been lifted from her. Her professional wins have grown exponentially because she is taking the same direct, honest approach in her business dealings that she's using in her personal life. The two were inextricably linked. She has all the proof she needs to continue on the path of self-respect and healthy boundaries going forward.

If reading all of this has made you question whether you yourself engage in toxic behavior, take heart. It means you have the self-awareness to recognize it. You have the opportunity to be very conscious and change the way you relate to others moving forward. Find a therapist who can help you evaluate where you are versus where you want to be.

To Don't:

- **Don't use logic in an attempt to overcome the manipulation tactics** of a toxic person. Logic and emotion are apples and oranges that can't be used to combat one another.
- **Don't give in for the sake of short-term peace.** It's not worth it, and you are playing into the hands of the toxic person each time you decide it's easier to go along.
- **Don't decide that it's harmless to continue participating in the cycle** of toxicity because you're aware of what's happening. It's not harmless. Your awareness is complicity in your own emotional injury.

Do Instead:

- **Establish boundaries.** Resist the urge to use logic when you get pushback.
- **Speak up.** Even if you aren't sure how to resolve the situation, silence is not the answer.
- **Know that you have the power** to break this cycle once and for all.

Summing Up

The presence of toxicity has the power to establish an undermining pattern that pervades every aspect of your life. It must be dealt with head-on, with an empowered approach in which your own best interests or the interests of a group lead the way. You can clean up every other aspect of your mindset and operating framework but not get the true benefits of those efforts until you are willing to stop tolerating behavior that hurts you or your team, assertively establish your expectations, and stick to the commitment that serves your highest good in staying strong when your expectations aren't met. If you are an enabler, it's time to take stock and admit your part in the dysfunction you have allowed. Acknowledge that your participation has effects beyond you, and, if needed, get outside help in sorting out how you got here so that you can move forward.

Remember:

- Toxic behavior can be obvious or subtle. Remember to watch for manipulation tactics that leverage FOG (Fear, Obligation, Guilt) to bend you to the will of the manipulator.
- Common toxic behaviors include non-apologies, refusal to accept responsibility, victim mindset, projection, lack of empathy, and passive aggression.
- A lack of boundaries is at the heart of what *enables* toxic behavior. The one who manipulates doesn't have limits in the area that they are intruding on. It is up to you to decide what you will no longer tolerate, set the rules, make the consequences clear, and then stay consistent and true to the limits you have set.
- Logic is a tool for people who behave rationally. Manipulation is an emotional technique—you cannot use logic to talk the manipulator out of their bad behavior. Setting and sticking to boundaries without rationalizing is the key to managing such relationships.
- It takes two to participate in a toxic interaction. The toxic person has found an enabler in you. Stop enabling, remove yourself from participation, and free yourself of the invasive

effect that ongoing interaction is having on every aspect of your life.

- Toxicity you tolerate shows up personally and professionally. You have to clean it all up to move forward, fully empowered to transform your life.

Take a deep breath. No matter how tough a toxic situation you're in, there is a way out. If you have more than one toxic situation in your life that needs to be addressed, begin with the one that is the least overwhelming to you. Perhaps the behavior in question is less egregious, or the relationship itself isn't as significant to you, so if the interaction gets rocky, it's less threatening to your peace of mind. This is a baby-steps approach that allows you to get in some practice asserting your boundaries and expectations, which will build your confidence, making it easier for you to approach the other, more significant relationships or behaviors that remain.

The following will help provide clarity on how to begin this process.

1. Make a list of your toxic relationships. Rank them in order of which are the most unsettling and painful for you.
2. For each of these people, think about the last interaction or two you've had. Identify the tactics they use to manipulate you. Don't worry about making an all-inclusive list. The point of this exercise is to raise your awareness of any subtleties you may not have been picking up on before.
3. Pick the relationship you are most comfortable starting with and come up with the boundaries you want to put in place. I encourage you to play out the interaction in your mind, thinking through their most likely responses and what you would say in return. Practicing your responses will minimize your anxiety when it comes time to have the interaction, making it less likely you'll be taken off-guard, unsure what to say in response to an objection.
4. Give yourself a deadline for having the conversation. If it's someone you see frequently, pick a date two to four weeks out and make it a priority to establish your boundaries with

this person. Having a timeline will give you time to think, practice, and prepare while creating a sense of urgency around having to be prepared.

5. Once you've addressed the first relationship, repeat the process for the others on your list. Enlist the help of those close to you by confiding in them about the true nature of your relationship. Chances are, you're telling them something they've already picked up on. They will want to support you in taking this critical step. With a particularly angry or volatile toxic personality, be cautious. Talk to your doctor or a therapist about your plan for moving forward and take their professional advice. Remember, you are not stuck. You do have options, and you can move forward from here. It may take a little more time and planning, but it's worth it. You're worth it.

6. Employ early identification with future relationships. When you see the warning signs of toxicity, do not engage! Your well-being comes first.

CHAPTER 3

Break the Chains

The programming that drives you, from your earliest experiences to the relationship dynamics that you've grown accustomed to, contributes to who you are and how you show up in the world. All patterns, whether positive or negative, have one thing in common—they lull you into autopilot mode. They are such a part of your daily life that you can pass through them unconsciously, not registering the mental and emotional impact a pattern is having on your life. Consider how you get to work each day. When you first started your job, you paid attention, as the drive was not quite second nature yet. You may have experimented with a couple of different routes to see which was better from a traffic and convenience perspective, then you likely never looked back. The best way was settled upon, and, from that point on, you've gotten to work the same way each day for days, weeks, and then years, the daily commute on repeat in a way that barely requires you to be conscious.

Your commute to work is a benign example, but what about the patterns that have real impact? If you don't become conscious of their presence and begin to examine where your default mode of operation is cruising along, you remain unaware of the ways in which how you operate isn't serving you and, in some cases, is actively sabotaging you.

Patterns can show up in a multitude of ways. They can be internal and subconscious, appearing as habitual ways of thinking, feeling, or responding to the world. Patterns can also show up in relation to others in the form of repeated experiences, personality types, and relationship scenarios. They are closely tied to your limiting beliefs and to the interpersonal dynamics you tolerate on a regular basis. Patterns are essentially the expression of your programming, and whatever remains unaddressed, you will find yourself repeating. The programming feedback loop will go on and on until you consciously put a stop to what isn't working for you and replace the pattern with a conscious, healthy way of showing up.

Is all programming bad? No, not necessarily. There is likely some programming that appears to work in your favor, at least on the surface. For instance, if part of your programming is that you don't quit, that has played a huge role in your high-achieving mode of operation. However, there is a potential dark side. If you equate quitting with failure, it will be much harder to step away from something, even when it's in your best interest to do so. As you begin to identify and recognize patterns of thought and behavior, it's imperative that you resist the urge to make snap decisions about whether a pattern is something that hurts or helps you (or some of both) before you've had time to consider all the angles.

Go Inside Your Head

Revisit your limiting beliefs from Chapter 1. How are they making an appearance in the form of patterns in your thought processes? Are you a worrier? What do you worry about? Are you afraid to fail? What do you tell yourself about what failure means? Do you avoid confrontation? What are the words in your head when you're backing down from a discussion or deciding not to put in your two cents? When something goes wrong, what is your mental response?

Let's consider worry to illustrate how a limiting belief can turn into a repetitive pattern.

Limiting belief: Nothing ever goes my way.

Thought: What a beautiful day. The baseball game will be fun.

Worry: What if it rains? It will have been a waste of time to go all the way out to the field, and what if the rescheduled time isn't convenient? I really don't want to have to go to a game this weekend, we have too much going on.

Pattern: Habitually expecting the worst and following that thought to its doom-and-gloom conclusion.

On the surface, this may seem like a fairly benign cascade of thoughts. If you take out the baseball-game scenario, you can see the underlying danger in the limiting belief and its associated pattern:

Nothing ever goes my way = I expect the worst

Worries big and small can reveal a wealth of information to you about your approach to life. When you apply the pattern generally, you can see the theme and how damaging it is to be in the cycle. How will you ever reach your full potential if you expect the worst? If you believe that things don't go your way, you not only convince yourself of a sucky outcome, you invite it.

Let's do this again with respect to self-worth to further demonstrate the impact of the link between limiting beliefs and patterns.

Limiting belief: I lack the discipline to follow through.

Thought: I want to create a process for my organization that will help streamline the way we interact with our clients.

Worry: I won't get the support I need. This is a big project that requires the input of others. Maybe I'm not up to the task.

Pattern: Retreating from opportunities due to fear of failure.

In this case, a programmed belief that you tend to leave projects incomplete due to a lack of discipline leads you to either back away from a challenge altogether, or leave it half-done because you lack the discipline to see it through. The impact of this limiting belief/pattern combo is:

I lack the discipline to follow through = I will fail

For each of these examples, you could plug in all kinds of different scenarios and still reach the same ultimate conclusions about how your limiting belief holds you in a self-defeating pattern. The extent to which these patterns are insidious and subconscious makes them difficult to identify. The key to that identification is to wake up. You must come out of autopilot mode, become conscious of how the things you tell yourself lead to the patterns that bind you, and strategically break down the thought process that keeps you stuck in the cycle. We will get into how to do that a little later on.

Dig into Your Relationships

The one-two punch of limiting beliefs and patterns isn't restricted to your internal world. The same combo has a major influence on how you relate to others, what you expect in relationships, what you tolerate, and how often you experience similar themes and challenges interpersonally. Relationship dynamics are subject to your personal limiting beliefs, with the added challenge that the other person's beliefs are also in the mix. That combination sets up a scenario in which you are contributing to the cycle, the other person is playing a role, and you establish a pattern in which the outward expression of your beliefs creates the dynamic in which you find yourself. Because you can't be inside the other person's head, you must focus on how you are feeding the dynamic and how you can address your part in it.

Limiting belief: I am not interesting.

Thought: I have to go to my work holiday party.

Worry: I dread social gatherings. What if I say the wrong thing or bore people?

Pattern: Avoiding interaction with others due to low self-confidence.

Belief of others: They don't like to be social, therefore we will leave them alone.

By now, I hope you've caught on to the extent to which your limiting beliefs and associated patterns create your reality. This example in particular shows clearly that this person's low self-esteem directly contributes to limited social contact:

I am uninteresting = I isolate myself

The people around you have no idea why you behave as you do. Often, they are simply following your lead and, in that way, giving you space to create the reality you're living in, even if it's not the reality you desire. The added danger here is that the pattern established by limiting beliefs can lead you down the slippery slope of believing you're a victim of circumstance or of the actions of others, rather than leading you to examine your own behavior and how you contribute to what you experience.

When it comes to your work life, the personal and relational dynamics at play establish deep ruts that you may have a hard time climbing out of. The extent to which you are the architect of your circumstances escapes you until you make a deliberate decision to cut the shit. No more effing around. Wake up, tune in, and decide that, right here and now, you have within you everything you need to break the chains that bind you.

Now that you have a few examples, let's get into some limiting belief/worry/pattern associations that commonly arise in professional scenarios so that you can add to this list with your own experiences in mind.

Limiting belief:	I'm not that smart.
Worry:	People will find out that I'm not smart.
Pattern:	I overwork or otherwise overcompensate to prove my value.

Limiting belief:	I'm not good enough.
Worry:	I'm going to lose my job.
Pattern:	I expect the worst.

Limiting belief:	There aren't enough hours in the day.
Worry:	I'll never get it all done.
Pattern:	I'm overwhelmed and unable to prioritize.

Limiting belief:	The world is an unfriendly place.
Worry:	Someone will try to hurt me.
Pattern:	I am defensive and suspicious.

The examples above demonstrate that there is no such thing as compartmentalization; any of these can apply to any or many areas of your life. Once you've identified one area, you will begin to see how the pattern shows up globally.

That last example regarding the unfriendliness of the world was one that had a serious impact on my life when I was just an adolescent. I grew up steeped in toxicity. Anger and expressions of rage, physical and verbal, were a regular and consistent part of life at home. From a very young age, I instinctively tuned in to the tension in my household that signaled it was best to stay away, and simultaneously internalized the belief that the world was not a safe place. I became guarded, defensive. I expected rage to be directed my way and became accustomed to doing everything I could to avoid it while remaining in a state of high alert.

When I look back on my childhood, I can easily call up the feelings of confusion and anger that were close to the surface so much of the time. My father's verbal and physical abuse went from scaring me as a small child to filling me with my own rage when I began to approach adolescence and had had enough of that bullshit, thank you. My rage prompted me to do not-very-smart things, like take my own swings at my father in retaliation, further fueling his rage and prolonging the battles. I didn't care. The only thing I wanted was to scream and hit him as hard as I could, and all too often, I did just that. Other times, I would silently seethe, full of unexpressed fury and sadness, just wanting him to go away. I knew that if I didn't react, it would be over more quickly. My experience at home seeped into the world outside and impacted my friendships and workplace relationships. I was on high alert with everyone, all the time. I expected that people would try to hurt me. It became a part of my operating system to walk around simmering with anger, ready to lash out defensively with rage if anyone dared to cross me.

My emotional state began to make itself known in my body. Around the age of sixteen, I started experiencing strange aches and pains that appeared consistently, day after day, for weeks at a time. Of course, I concluded that I must have cancer and was going to die soon (expecting the worst!), so I went to see my family physician. After examining me and finding nothing amiss, he asked if it was possible that I could be depressed. The question surprised me. I had never had symptoms of depression as I understood them at that point in my life. I knew my dad was chronically depressed, and that my mom sometimes battled it, but I didn't feel disengaged. I certainly wasn't suicidal. I was still hanging out with friends, doing well in school, going to work, and generally doing everything I always had. My physician told me that it's not unusual for unexplained pain to be a symptom of depression. I thought about my home life and how much more difficult the dynamics of my family relationships were becoming as I got older. Yes, depression was a possibility. He offered to write a prescription if I needed short-term relief. I opted for a referral instead. I wasn't opposed to medication but wanted to give therapy a chance, since I hadn't even been consciously aware of my mental/emotional state and how it might be contributing to the pain manifesting in my body.

I had no idea what to expect at my first visit, but the professorial type, wearing his sweater with elbow patches and sporting slightly rumpled hair, set me at ease. He was soft-spoken and thoughtful. We talked a lot about my anger. I told him I felt like a trapped animal, hanging out in my corner, hackles up, hissing in warning until someone provoked me. I spent a lot of time in a defensive state, knowing it was a matter of when, not if, I would be hassled in some way I would have to defend against. I shared this with the therapist to the best of my ability, hoping he understood what I was trying to convey.

He asked, "*Why* are you angry?"

Um. Had he not been listening? I thought I had already answered that question. I told him so, and his response was one that has stuck with me ever since.

He said, "Anger is a secondary emotion. It is a defensive response to a deeper, more painful emotion. What's the deeper feeling below your anger?"

This question blew my mind wide open. Not only did it have profound implications for me, it also changed the lens through which I viewed my parents. I had to mull it over.

It turned out that beneath my anger was hurt. Hurt, and a sense of betrayal that the people who were supposed to love me the most consistently let me down. Instead of keeping me safe, they chose to keep indulging their lower impulses, to look away (as I felt was the case with extended family members), to blame me for their rage. Thus, my belief that the world was an unfriendly place was established. The only tools available to me at the time were those I had witnessed in my parents, so I adopted their anger and made it my own way of dealing.

Limiting beliefs about yourself and the world, and the patterns that go with them, can be passed down to you ancestrally. My parents' own experiences were that the world was an unfriendly place. My mother lost her father when she was ten years old. My father had endured abuse from his own father as a child. They were angry and defensive in order to protect themselves. They were in their feedback loops and wouldn't break free, whereas I desperately wanted to find another way, one which allowed me some peace of mind and an ability to step away from the exhausting defensive posture I maintained inside my head.

Interrupt the Pattern

How did I break free? By waking up, taking stock, gaining understanding, and deciding I was done. When anger welled up, I would stop and ask myself why I felt threatened. What was happening in that moment that made me feel unsafe? What was I trying to protect against? Interrupting the cycle by taking a pause, rather than going straight into the pattern, is the key to breaking it. Putting the brakes on your habitual reaction, by stopping to assess how you're about to react and why, is just enough of a disruption to take you into a totally different mental place. It takes you from reactivity to thoughtful contemplation. This pause gives you a moment to consider how you can choose a different reaction from a place of consciousness rather than unconsciousness. In my own process, anger had become such a natural reaction that simply taking a moment to think it over was enough to defuse my agitation. In my calmer state, I could appreciate why I was about to react in the old way and choose to react more appropriately in a given situation. The answer wasn't always the same, which helped me stay present. I couldn't just have *the* answer that would allow me to slide right back into a pattern. I had to be tuned in to myself and the situation.

As discussed in the programming chapter, limiting beliefs are rarely true; they are simply beliefs. The most effective way to interrupt patterns is to repeatedly poke holes in the "logic" that was used to construct them until you drain the power of the initial belief.

In my example, that could look something like this:

Limiting belief: The world is an unfriendly place.

Belief interruptions: The world is what I make of it. I am safe. The world is an awesome place.

Worry: Someone will try to hurt me.

Worry interruptions: I can take care of myself. I surround myself with good people.

Pattern: I am defensive and suspicious.

Pattern after consistent interruptions: I am thoughtful and self-reflective.

There is no need to rush out and take full inventory of every nook and cranny of your life. It's enough to start with a couple of patterns, work to interrupt and reprogram those, then move on to others. Like every other personal development activity, this muscle needs to be flexed over time until the process becomes second nature to you. Once it has, you will more quickly and easily pick up on patterns that need to be addressed and will be equipped to address them efficiently and deliberately.

If you're feeling stumped about where to begin, the most straightforward approach is to be on the alert for situations and relationship patterns that seem to show up over and over again. Is there a scenario at work that shows up repeatedly? Maybe you had a difficult coworker or boss that prompted you to switch teams, only to find the new team has someone just like the person you tried to escape? Personally, maybe you've left a relationship or marriage, entered another, and found that the things that didn't work for you before are still an issue, despite having connected with someone new. Any time you ask yourself "Why does this keep happening to me?" or "How do I keep ending up here?" is your wake-up call to PAY ATTENTION. Anything you do not address, you are doomed to repeat. If you left a situation without sufficient self-reflection and a willingness to accept your part in what you experienced, you will find yourself in the same situation again. It's easy to fall into the trap of feeling sorry for yourself or bewildered by the cyclic nature of what you experience. Instead, realize:

The pattern is not happening *to* you. It's happening *for* you.

When a pattern shows up yet again, it's to provide you with another opportunity to address it in a way that helps you grow, rather than avoid. You are not perfect. You make mistakes, trigger people, overlook details, participate rather than speak up—in other words, you're a human being. Avoiding hard truths in order to protect yourself or another person will backfire on all involved. There is no forward movement when you refuse to be uncomfortable and do the work to overcome the cycle. The point of all this self-awareness is to make you see in no uncertain terms just how much you participate in holding yourself back. It's much harder to retreat into denial when you're awake and tuned in. If you choose to do nothing, the knowledge will nag at you, making you so uncomfortable that your only choice is to take the steps needed to address the situation. Once you do, the empowerment and relief that follow will energize you to address the other patterns that are keeping you stuck.

To Don't:

- Don't believe you can **compartmentalize your life**. It doesn't work. What affects one area of your life affects them all.
- **Don't operate on autopilot.** If you stay unconscious, you'll stay right where you are.
- **Don't get overwhelmed** at the thought of all the patterns you need to address. It will take some time to rework the way you operate.

Do Instead:

- **WAKE UP. Be conscious**, stay curious, and begin to recognize the cycles you are in and how they impact you.
- **Interrupt patterns with a thought or mental statement** that weakens the pattern (tips below in chapter summary).
- **Remember that the pattern is happening for you, not to you.** Its continuous presence is meant as a call to action. Once you address it, the pattern no longer has power over you.

Summing Up

The patterns in your life are a natural extension of your limiting beliefs and interpersonal experiences. They may originate with you or be passed down ancestrally, establishing a multi-generational belief system and pattern that affects your entire family. In order to break free of the patterns in your life, you have to get out of autopilot mode, become conscious, and commit to interrupting any given pattern consistently until it is broken. While it may sound like a lot of work, keep in mind that it's taken your entire life to get to where you are. The good news is that, with a few weeks of focus, you can make tremendous progress in disrupting the patterns that no longer serve you. After a few months, you'll find that you naturally tune in and disrupt patterns as they come to your awareness. As a result, you will feel empowered and energized to continue on your personal development journey, having broken free from the mental chains that have been holding you back.

Grab your journal and consider the following to get started with pattern disruption.

1. Revisit the limiting belief exercise from Chapter 1 and begin filling in the trifecta of limiting belief/worry/pattern, as described previously, for each of your beliefs. For example:

   Limiting belief: There aren't enough hours in the day.
   Worry: I don't have time to do everything on my list.
   Pattern: ?

   At first, you may not know how the pattern is showing up, and that's perfectly okay. Going from limiting belief to how that shows up in your worries or thoughts will plant the seed in your mind, and the pattern will reveal itself to you as you remain tuned in. When you have a realization, come back and fill in the gaps. You may have more than one pattern for any limiting belief/worry combo. In this scenario, potential patterns could be a state of chronic overwhelm, consistently working into the night to get it all done, feeling behind the eight ball, etc.

2. Expand upon your limiting beliefs by identifying the mental habits that don't serve you. Bad mental habits include being angry/defensive, feeling victimized/ganged up on, needing to prove yourself, seeking recognition, retreating, quitting, resigning yourself, etc. The habits themselves may represent a pattern to tune into. Once you've identified these habits, come up with the limiting beliefs that underlie them.
3. Create pattern interruptions for yourself. Keep them short and to the point. With particularly insidious patterns, write your interruptions down on a Post-It Note and put it where you will see it frequently. Your car's dashboard, your bathroom mirror, or your laptop or desk are ideal, as you can quickly take a glance when you need to redirect your thoughts. Some examples:

    - Limiting belief: I'm undisciplined.
    - Interruption: I am capable and competent.

    - Limiting belief: There isn't enough time.
    - Interruption: I have all the time I need to address my priorities.

    - Limiting belief: I'll never lose the weight.
    - Interruption: I can do anything I commit myself to.

4. Buddy up and work through this with a friend or partner if you find it challenging to get started. You can catalyze the process by sharing the patterns you see in each other, talking through the beliefs, and coming up with good interruptions to address them.

PART II

Meet Your Operating System

CHAPTER 4

To Achieve or Not to Achieve

When I was a little kid, I was all about speed. I wanted to see how fast I could do just about anything. I loved those games in school where we'd race each other at the blackboard, furiously solving arithmetic problems as quickly as possible. The one who solved the fastest got to stay at the board and take on the next challenger. I was often the one who got to stay up there the longest, getting a little jolt of satisfaction and pride with each kid I took down with my razor-sharp—and speedy!—addition and subtraction skills. I took that competitive edge into everything I did, wanting to be the fastest and the best. On the playground, I made sure I left people in the dust when it came time to race. Kids would actually pick me to race against so they would be challenged to bring their A game. After I learned how to ride my bike, I would race against myself, seeing how fast I could take corners and how many laps I could do around the square grassy area in front of our townhome. If there was an opportunity to prove myself, I took it.

The need to prove myself stayed with me for years and years. The double-edged sword for me was that the achievement of "winning" over and over again created a feedback loop, one that reinforced the idea that winning was good, because, wasn't it exhilarating every single time? And wasn't it cool to be known for the things that I kicked ass at, even if just for a little while? Of course, there is absolutely nothing wrong with enjoying competition and getting a charge from winning. When we are young, that positive reinforcement shows us what we are capable of, gives us a sense of what we can achieve, and drives us to continue to excel in the areas of particular interest for each of us. It could be sports, art, music, academics, and, once we are older, work as well.

Our own experiences program us to conceptualize success and are compounded by the societal and external messages we receive about what it takes to be successful, and why success is something you should strive for. So much of what we hear and are shown emphasizes the grind of creating success. What does it take?

- Hard work!
- Never saying no to additional responsibility!
- Working on your weaknesses!
- Hustling!

Generally, you've been taught that you'd better bust your ass if you want to be successful, and further, it's implied here that your needs outside of the pursuit are not central to the success equation. Do what you're told, take on more, focus on what's wrong with you, and success is yours for the taking. Is it any wonder that success achieved by these means feels hollow and unfulfilling?

As if all of that wasn't enough, the industry you're in has a huge impact on how you perceive success. If your industry is attached to struggle, you get further reinforcement that the work you do, and the best way to do it, is *haaaard*. Working long shifts? Great! Shift work is totally noble, and you should wear your exhaustion like a badge of honor. Busting out your laptop after dinner and working long into the night? Awesome! When your boss sees that email you sent at one in the morning, he'll know what a badass you are, because who needs sleep when you could be working? Your company wants you to take that certification exam that requires ten hours of class on weeknights for the next six weeks? Fab! You don't need to go to the gym or see your family anyway. The ways in which demands are made on our time and energy are nearly endless, and worse yet, our programming obligates us to meet those demands, no matter how taxing they may be on us personally. It's easy to rationalize by telling yourself that the latest demand is a one- or limited-time thing, but the likelihood that additional demands will continue to roll in is very high, and before you know it, you're on the effort treadmill, relentlessly setting your own needs aside in pursuit of "success."

Chances are the success you are striving for is largely defined by the world around you. You've learned through experience and absorption that success is measured by the following:

- Adhering to the rules as they've been laid out for you by your programming, industry, and societal norms
- Achieving the tangible and measurable by checking the boxes on goals, seeing the money in your bank account, and having the title that conveys status
- Sticking to formulas, e.g. acting in accordance with the results of the latest personality test, following the advice of people who tell you when to wake up and what the most productive time of day is, emulating the other successful people you see so that you, too, can be a high-achieving machine

But what if you've already done all or most of this? Are you fulfilled by what you've achieved? Why are you bored, apathetic, restless, exhausted, irritated, etc.? Because the tangible is rarely fulfilling. When you are focused on gathering what can be measured, you completely overlook what cannot be measured. The key to a fulfilling life lies within the intangibles that you have overlooked and deprioritized.

One of the most pervasive and damaging societal expectations we internalize is the idea that we should know what we want to create for our lives at the age of eighteen. Eighteen?! We expect fledgling adults to pick a topic and stick with it for four years or longer, then go into the world, get the j-o-b, work until retirement, and then maybe they can do something they're really interested in. There is a measure of practicality here, absolutely. You must start somewhere to get going in life, no doubt. That in and of itself is not the problem. The problem is the ridiculous expectation that once you've picked something, you will stick with it. Longevity is celebrated, and too bad for you that the rewards for the time invested don't come until much, much later in life. Inherent in this philosophy is that you must put in your time to deserve the freedom you're creating for the future. Making it through the grind is part of the journey, so you better put your head down and get it done.

The generations that preceded us had this messaging in spades, and they stayed in line with expectations, not because they were thrilled by their nine-to-five, but because there were actually fewer career options available in their time than we have in ours. Technology has triggered a massive shift in the way we do business, and we see more and more people who are working for themselves, leveraging social media and online technology to create lucrative businesses, taking a risk on entrepreneurship to see if they can make it work for a shot at freedom and a non-corporate lifestyle. However, the majority of people working in the corporate machinery are still steeped in the outdated messaging and surrounded by people who have accepted (or resigned themselves to) the way it works, determined to stay the course because the benefits and pay are good, and a little boredom and apathy is a small price to pay to have checked the boxes of success. They can enjoy life in fifteen to twenty years when they retire.

The first time it occurred to me that it might be time to consider a different line of work was about halfway through my corporate career. I had a good run of several years before that, where I focused on the esoteric subject of genetics while learning a tremendous amount about healthcare information technology. It's a highly complex area, and I was energized by the continuous cycle of learning, as I'm a natural student at heart. There was so much I didn't know, and it was like I had hit the job jackpot; my work had enough complexity in it to keep me engaged. For someone prone to boredom like I am, that was a huge benefit for me. What made the company seem to the outside world like a hard place to work was this element of complexity, and an expectation that those who came on board would be up to the task of navigating that complexity with limited guidance. You had to be a self-starter to be effective, and if you wanted to differentiate yourself, you had to connect with the right people in the right places. I had the appetite for both, and thus began a highly expansive time for me, one in which I was energized by work, the challenge, and the prospect of rising in the ranks. I remember thinking how lucky I was to have found "my place," at that point feeling certain that I would spend the rest of my career there.

I had a pretty long honeymoon period, though those first few years were far from perfect. At the time, I compartmentalized the aspects of my work that bothered me, able to do so fairly easily because I was otherwise energized by my position. Over time, it became harder to overlook the unhealthy elements of corporate life. I'm a direct communicator and that was an issue for some, especially some men. I was repeatedly advised to tone down my style, which rankled the shit out of me. The same behavior in men was celebrated rather than criticized. The founders of the company were a trio of older men, all of whom had reputations for being fond of the ladies. There was no policy against dating within the company; the only exception was that people on the same team should not be involved with one another. Otherwise, you'd see and hear all kinds of crazy things, the most common being that a man or woman in a position of power would form a dalliance with a subordinate, and the gossip mill would churn gleefully at a rapid clip, spreading the news far and wide and generally creating an atmosphere in which power meant you could do as you pleased, and certainly that you were entitled to such behavior if you had the right title after your name. There were far more men than women known for this behavior, which contributed to the undertone of sexism and the sense that, as a woman, you might be tolerated better if you adopted stereotypical behavior that was non-threatening to the delicate sense of superiority that the men had cultivated. At the very least, you should be careful not to appear combative.

If any of this sounds familiar to you, aren't you tired? The spoken and unspoken expectations will rule your life and turn you into a horse with blinders on, an otherwise powerful being whose gaze is being trained to focus on those things deemed important by those in authority, robbing you of your ability to move fully under your own power in the direction that you choose. And here's the really sticky wicket in all of this—it's that you are participating by lining up to have said blinders put on, limiting your vision and the pursuit of that which lights you up. Until you truly stop to consider it, you don't fully comprehend just how close the guard rails are to this path that you're walking. It's unlikely you will have a sudden realization where all the pieces fall into place all at once, even if you accept that you're wearing blinders. What is more likely is that you'll start to feel stagnant as the result of this limited focus.

Redefining Success

Success that requires your acquiescence to staying limited must be redefined. The sheer amount of settling you must do to get to this place is terrible for your sense of self-worth, and the sabotage happens in often subtle ways, at a slow enough pace that you can go years without realizing the effect all this settling is having on you. What version of success are you adhering to that requires you to settle in order to have it?? Settling does not equal success. Further, it's not practical to assume you can continue to exist in this state indefinitely. Ever heard of burnout? A quick refresher:

> **Burnout:** physical or mental collapse caused by overwork or stress.

When you spend so much time achieving and meeting the demands that are thrust upon you without stopping to consider yourself and what you need, assuming that there are no other options, you will burn out. Worse yet, if you have ascended to your place in the organization by adopting that approach, you've engaged in a feedback loop where your role as a cog in the great machine has been rewarded and recognized, making it that much harder to consider an alternative. It is far better to stop, assess, and determine where you are subjugating your own needs before you get to the point of burnout. Whether that tipping point is mental and you fall into depression or physical and you have a heart attack, neither is a desirable scenario and either will set you back dramatically, if not kill you outright. These are not viable options. When they occur, they are crises that demand your attention and will force you to see what you are doing to yourself when it's almost, or already, too late.

Now that you're convinced your personal definition of success requires an upgrade, it's time to get clear on the ways in which you've resigned yourself to the definition as you've known it.

This was one of the most eye-opening experiences I had when I started considering my situation. It didn't take long for me to understand why I was stuck, restless, and honestly frightened by the prospect of not having an alternative to consider. When I began to consider looking at outside opportunities, picturing myself in a new environment, likely with a nice title and salary, it didn't feel that great. I tried to sweeten the prospect by adding in thoughts of a shorter commute which would allow me to leave home a little later, to have more time with the kids in the morning, and to make it to the gym mid-day and would generally relieve a little of the time pressure that was my constant companion. My mental assessment of those improvements had less of an impact than I had hoped. It took me from a one to maybe a five on the scale of perceived improvement, which was unpleasantly surprising. I had always believed that having more time and a bit more freedom were the underlying motivators for making a change. Clearly, they were valuable and led to minor improvement to the bigger picture, but they were not nearly as powerfully motivating as I had expected. That's when things got even scarier.

Having the nice pros checklist was a decent place to start. I had to consider what about my current situation could be better, and doing so brought me to the point where I could actually see with much greater clarity that the deal-sweeteners I'd been throwing in weren't all that powerful. Knowing that forced me to go deeper, to continue the exercise of considering my options and what would actually energize me and bring me out of the land of "meh." Making a change that included some benefits was fine but felt like too much of a baby step. I was certain that, within a few years, I would be right back where I had started, wondering why fulfillment continued to elude me.

What it came down to was my willingness to compromise. What was I willing to give up in favor of improvement? Could I stay put, find the areas where I could compromise and work on the areas where I would not? I understood with crystal clarity that my work environment was far from unique; chances are you relate to much of what I've shared, and I don't know the specifics of where you work or your industry. There are pieces of corporate culture that can be found in any company, big or small, new or old, and across industries. Ultimately, that understanding was what kept me from being too excited about a change of scenery. I knew that there would be surface differences at a new place, but the underlying mechanics might be so similar as to be indistinguishable from what and why I had left.

The scenery was not the issue. The people were not the issue. The industry wasn't the issue. Me, myself, and I was the issue. I craved something more. I had all the tangible success I could handle. It was something intangible that I was chasing—to feel as if I provided value and could move through the world with purpose. And quite frankly, I was sick of being the center of my own universe. I wanted the opportunity to contribute to the well-being of others, and the cycle I was in left no actual mental or emotional time and space in which to consider how I could make that a significant theme in my life. A job change wasn't going to provide me with what I really wanted. It was far too difficult to mentally construct what my ideal work/life purpose scenario would look like, so instead I focused on a broader redefinition of success that included what was missing at the time.

As I considered the intangible elements that would become central to my personal construct of success, I started by thinking about the intangibles that made my life not so awesome. My early tendency in this attempt was to get too specific and checkbox-y (my redefinition attempts were highly susceptible to my programming!), so I decided to back off and start as simply as possible.

Don't Want	**Want Instead**
Scattered thoughts, lack of mental clarity	Clear focus
Relentlessly scheduled	Time flexibility
Anxious, irritable	Peace of mind
Self-focus	Generosity
Concern about money and spending	Prosperity
Isolation	Connectedness

Notice how this entire list, on both sides, consists of the intangible. None of these things can be measured in any specific way, but moving from the "don't want" to the "want" column would create a massive shift in the way I felt about my life on a daily basis. Having clarity regarding the intangibles I wanted more of allowed me to come up with tangible ways to create each of those things. Here's how I approached each of these to get to the desired state:

- Clear focus—journaling, daily five-minute meditations, conscious effort to clear the clutter in my mind to make way for clarity.
- Time flexibility—visualizing what a career/lifestyle with flexibility would feel like. Notice here that I didn't focus on *how* to create such flexibility, but rather what my days would be like if I had the kind of flexibility I craved.
- Peace of Mind—brainstorming ways to reduce the anxiety through specific acts like taking walks, reading, journaling, while again visualizing and feeling what a life with less anxiety would feel like.
- Generosity and Prosperity—expressing deliberate gratitude for all that I had and experienced every day. If I was paying a bill, I was sending out gratitude for the service that was provided in exchange for that money. Instead of allowing guilt to interfere with the thought of scheduling a massage, I would express gratitude for the money that enabled me to experience enjoyment and relaxation.
- Connectedness—looking for ways to expand my network and connect with new people every month. If someone asked me to meet for a drink or coffee, I would say yes, and I extended my own invitations as well. My focus was on meeting people outside of my industry and social circle.

The framework for a life that felt different, *better*, began to take shape as I spent time on these exercises. I was working full-time and still immersed in the stress of my life at the time, but it was a daily priority for me to spend time on journaling and mind-clearing, whether it was taking a walk outside or meditating for a few minutes. It took a couple of weeks to become part of my natural rhythm, but once it did, I looked forward to spending the time alone, and got really excited about the rate at which I was filling up my journal with realizations and thoughts of the future. I still write nearly every single day; the writing itself is like an evolution of my meditation practice, where I clear my mind of all but that which I'm focused on. It was empowering to have an idea of what to work toward, and even though having that map didn't necessarily tell me how to get there, it was as if I had found the tools I needed to make it to the next step. The list of wants also played an incredibly important role as a decision aid. When a new opportunity or avenue opened up, I could quickly assess it against my want list, and if it didn't contribute to the creation of that sensation, the answer was no. It streamlined the process of consideration, making the aligned decisions more obvious by removing the mystery from the equation. If it wasn't in alignment with what I had prioritized, it was a no. Easy. It allowed me to mentally move on, ready for the next opportunity to present itself so I could apply the process again.

To Don't:

- **Don't adhere to the rules and formulas of "success"** as they've been laid out by societal and industry-specific norms, especially when struggle is integral to those formulas.
- **Don't focus on the measurable at the cost of the priceless.**
- **Don't spend more time working through your weaknesses than appreciating your strengths.**

Do Instead:

- **Get clear on how your current version of success isn't serving you.** It's not, or you wouldn't be here.
- **Keep your highest good in mind.** It's time to make the turn away from meeting the expectations of others and toward what works for you personally.
- **Make decisions with *your* version of success in mind.** If an opportunity isn't aligned with what you want to create moving forward, it's a no. Engaging in this process of checking for alignment and passing on what will not work for you will continue to create greater clarity as you move forward.

Summing Up

The way you define success can hold you in a gilded cage of your own making, or it can set you free of the chains that you've allowed to bind you. Your only job right now is to tweak or change your definition of success so that it enables you to expand and grow, rather than settle and stagnate. When the analytical part of your brain tries to kick in and shut you down because the "how" is unclear, gently dismiss the thought and remind yourself that how you get there is not your concern at this moment. Your decision-making will evolve to accommodate your new definition of success; opportunities can be weighed in terms of how closely they align with where you want to go, rather than where you've been. Over time, you will become accustomed to thinking in terms of your highest good, and you will determine your next steps with clarity and relative ease, having removed the element of reactivity by being intentional about what you are moving toward.

Remember:

- Your current definition of success is likely riddled with elements that equate to struggle. These external messages that have come from family, friends, society, and your industry have been internalized, but they are not necessarily reflective of what you would choose for yourself.
- You have the power to change what you accept and to determine where you will compromise and what you will demand that is different than your status quo. It doesn't necessarily mean you have to quit your job, so relax and take the pressure off. This is about clarity, not immediate action.
- We tend to apply the construct of success to our professional lives and neglect how success feels in our personal lives. There is no way to separate the two, because we don't have split personalities. You can't leave your work at the office, and, if you've been telling yourself you can, it's time to stop. Clearly that is not the case, or you wouldn't be looking to recalibrate so you can have more of what fulfills you personally, rather than continuously striving for professional achievement.

Begin the process of examining what success means to you today and what isn't working, and start creating your new framework. Contemplate the following questions and flow with your responses. Allowing a stream of consciousness is a great way to get going with this exercise. You can always come back to refine things after you mentally vomit it all onto the page.

1. What about your life isn't working today? Try to focus on the intangible, e.g. your feelings about what could be better. It's okay to start with tangibles and then examine why the tangible in question isn't working for you, or how it makes you feel. For instance, if one of the status quo elements that isn't working for you is working long hours, ask yourself how that makes you feel. Exhausted? Disconnected from friends or family? Depressed? Frustrated? Get to the heart of the matter by focusing on the physical, mental, or emotional impact that piece of your life is having on you.
2. Once you have your list, start thinking about how you'd like to feel instead, as I showed in my own example earlier in the chapter. For example, if exhaustion is an issue for you right now, perhaps you want to feel energized, relaxed, or invigorated instead. Perhaps part of that is working fewer hours, but if you immediately go to the solution in that manner, chances are you'll start jamming yourself up by spiraling into just how you're going to reduce your hours, what it's going to take, how it's not possible, etc. Focusing on how you want to feel relieves the pressure of trying to figure out right this instant how you're going to get there. It's your desired state, period. Details are not required at this point.
3. Jot down your new list on a few Post-It Notes and put them up where you'll see them frequently. You are, after all, working on reprogramming, so the more you inundate yourself with the new program, the faster you'll get to where you want to be. It helps you remain conscious about the change you're creating, and it also works on your subconscious in that, whether or not you are actively reading these messages to yourself, your brain is taking them

in whenever they are visible and further enabling the shift. Stick notes on the dashboard of your car, on your laptop or monitor, your bathroom mirror, generally wherever you'll be exposed to the messages frequently.

4. From that point forward, use the new desired state you've envisioned as your decision aid. When you have to decide whether to take on a new project, add yet another thing to your plate, or examine new opportunities, do the analysis to see whether the thing in question aligns with your new priorities or not. If not, the answer should be an easy and firm "no." You may waver the first few times you attempt this new way of making decisions, but that's perfectly natural, as your old programming is still very much intact and just beginning to make way for the new. Stay consistent and it will become easier over time.

CHAPTER 5

How Fear Has Made You Its Bitch

Fear. A familiar feeling. It's been with you every step of the way. It was there when you were afraid to jump off the merry-go-round as a child, the moment you thought you might throw up before getting on the roller coaster for the first time, that time the teacher made you speak in front of the class, and so many more times, too numerous to count or remember. The feeling of fear is visceral, a primal biological and emotional response so distinctive, it can't be mistaken when you're young and operating from a more purely instinctual and primitive place.

Before we dive into the pitfalls that come with fear, let's go back to the beginning of time and think about the positive aspects, without which we would not have made it this far. Fear serves a critical purpose: survival. It heightens our awareness, alerts us to physical danger, prepares our bodies for fight or flight—it tries to ensure that we stay alive. Back in the caveman days, fear of creepy, dangerous things like poisonous snakes, insects, or giant animals that could eat you in a single bite was a very reasonable thing. You see a rattlesnake, you quickly turn and run in the opposite direction. You see a wasp's nest, you very slowly and quietly back away until you can freely run, screaming in panic, away from said nest. Fear of arousing the interest of beings that could hurt you serves the purpose of keeping you safe. This kind of fear saves your hide on a regular basis.

This same fear-based survival instinct played a role in how members participated in a community or tribe. If you wanted to survive the elements, you needed to run with a crew. Some members would hunt, others would care for children, some stood sentry while others rested. The likelihood of survival was greatly increased by belonging to a group. It was highly unlikely that a member of such a group would think, "No one here gets me. I'm out." The focus was on living to see another day, not emotional or spiritual fulfillment. Survival was the ultimate goal.

Because it can mean the difference between life and death, fear is a critical primal response, one that you are born with and that will stick with you until you draw your last breath. What makes it tricky to navigate is that it can be very difficult to differentiate between the useful kind of fear that keeps you alive and the limiting kind of fear that keeps you stuck where you are. Fear feels both yucky and compelling in its quest to keep you from making moves and taking risks. To further complicate matters, physiologically, your body doesn't differentiate between actual life-threatening fear and fear of, let's say, getting on stage. In our non-caveman modern experience, the kind of fear we experience on a regular basis isn't the life-threatening variety; you will have the same adrenaline-soaked reaction whether you're in actual danger or not. And that, my friends, is how the power of fear compels you.

As you get older and less primally driven, fear multiplies its impact by joining forces with ego. Fear and your ego become best friends, holding hands and skipping around inside your head with a baseball bat, ready to clobber you whenever you think of doing something outside your safe little box. Now, let's first be clear about something: the ego is not your enemy. We all have one, and it does indeed serve a purpose. There's a lot of spiritual messaging out there about transcending the ego, leaving it behind, etc., but I don't ascribe to that philosophy on the role of the ego. It does serve you, but it must evolve as part of the personal development process. When it hasn't evolved sufficiently, its single-minded mission is to keep you safe, even if it does so by invoking—you guessed it—fear.

This is why Fear and Ego are besties; they share a unified purpose. Your ego loves to pipe up in the form of a naysayer, telling you that it's not a good idea to pursue something, that you're not good enough, and it's even sneaky enough to use the language others have used against you (see Chapter 1) in its quest to keep the status quo just as it is, thank you. Perhaps the status quo is far from awesome, but it's known, and the devil you know is better than the one you don't, at least as far as your ego is concerned.

Fear and your ego have good intentions. But enough is enough. They are no longer welcome in the driver's seat. It's time for you to take the wheel.

First, you must accept that fear is going to show up. Your quest is to act in spite of it. When fear shows up, instead of heeding its call to take shelter and hide, examine it. What, exactly, is this fear trying to protect you from? Rejection? Anger? Dismissal? Visibility? Fear is just trying to be your friend. Fear thinks it's keeping you safe.

But fuck safe, already. Safe is how you stay stuck. Safe is not the zone of growth. Safe is the zone of the same ol', same ol'. In other words, bo-ring. Mundane. The stuff midlife crises are made of. Not where you want to be. And really, as a high achiever, how is it that you can be so intelligent, talented, and hard-working, and yet allow fear to hold such power over your actions? We will get into what to do when fear surfaces, but first, let's cover the predominant ways that fear shows up in disguise.

Three Illusions Fueled by Fear

Fear has a few tried and true ways of keeping you in your box. I like to call these the three illusions. We believe and operate as if these are actual things that can hurt us, when in reality, they are like sinister mirages in the desert that we swear we can see and want to avoid, yet as we get closer, they disappear. Let's talk about these illusions fueled by fear and how to flip your perspective so that they no longer keep you from moving forward.

Fear-Fueled Illusion 1: Failure

You might be thinking, what? How is failure not a real thing? Let's start by considering what kind of world we'd be living in if failure was an option that people universally adopted as the end of a venture. Here is an incredibly modest list of things you've come to rely upon or take for granted that would not exist today:

- The light bulb.
- Air travel.
- Modern medicine. All of it. Vaccines, antibiotics, surgical procedures, imaging technology, etc., etc.
- Computers.
- Cell phones.
- Clean drinking water.
- Elite athletes.
- Uh. Almost everything.

Failure is *never* the end of the line. It's an opportunity. To assess what you could have done differently. To really look at yourself and ask the tough questions like, "Did I really show up? Did I hold myself back in some way? Did I believe in myself? Did I believe in what I was trying to accomplish? Do I want this? What can I do next time? How can I tweak the process?" The questions you can ask, and the lessons you can learn, are nearly infinite. You don't have to be exhaustive in determining the root cause, but you do have to be willing to look at why something didn't go the way you hoped or expected it would. I guarantee that there is always something you can take from that experience so you can do something differently next time.

Let me give you a personal example. It was a professional mission of mine to reach the executive level in my corporate career. You might be wondering WTF I was thinking, having read my story at the beginning of this book, but remember, that was before I was "woke," as the cool kids like to say. It should have been easy for me. I had been promoted consistently, achieved "outstanding" status on several annual reviews, and had many of the right higher-ups supporting me and believing I could fill that role competently. It didn't happen.

The first time I thought I would be considered for executive promotion, the leader who promised to put my name in for consideration never did. She just…didn't. She also didn't bother to tell me she hadn't, instead sending my manager to have that awkward conversation with me. My supportive manager decided she was going to work hard to make it happen in the next review cycle and gave me every opportunity to showcase my abilities and results. Of course, by the time all of this was in the works, I was pretty sure that I was going to have to leave my job. Because I had been working to redefine what success meant for me personally, I was more aware than I had ever been in my life that reaching that level would not make me happy. I didn't see anyone at that level who was leading a life I admired or aspired to. In fact, it was quite the opposite. They didn't seem fulfilled. They were frustrated, disempowered, and appeared to be trapped. They were so much a part of the systemic dysfunction that, even if the will was there to create improvement, they either stopped trying after a while, didn't try at all, thinking the effort was futile, or worse yet, didn't even see that anything needed to change. Why had I ever thought I wanted that?

In the second-review-cycle attempt, my promotion came up for consideration. And it was blocked. I was told vaguely that an executive that I had butted heads with in the past had objected, saying I didn't have what it took, that I wasn't the right kind of person for the job—my read is that I wasn't willing to sell out and march to the corporate beat, therefore I was undesirable in that capacity. It wasn't hard to glean that meaning after years of having been told in no uncertain terms that the key to corporate success was to be less "me."

Hence, my goal of reaching the executive level failed. Failed?

Not from my perspective. Maybe you wouldn't be reading these words if I had "successfully" reached that goal.

Would I have changed my mind about leaving if I had gotten the promotion? Even though it's easy to say no from where I sit today, I'll never really know the answer to that question. But the way it went down flung open the door, showing me in no uncertain terms it was time to exit, stage left. It was the hand at my back I needed to free myself of the gilded cage I had willingly stayed in for years and years. It was not failure. It was opportunity. And because I had done so much personal development work by the time this "failure" took place, I recognized it for exactly what it was: an exhilarating, somewhat terrifying, Get Out of Jail Free card. So, I took it.

We all have these experiences, events, or situations from our past that, at the time, felt like devastating failures, that over time we've come to realize served a purpose. Hindsight is 20/20, right? The key is to not need an experience to be in the rearview in order to realize it has a purpose that is serving you. It's time to reframe the way you think about failure. Come up with a list of situations from the past that you initially perceived as failures but that, over time, you were able to see occurred for your benefit. How did you feel about them then? How do you feel about them now? If you can easily come up with more, write down as many examples as you can think of. Keep them in your journal or type them up and print out your list. This list will serve as your reality check when the fear of failure shows up to taunt you, reminding you that whatever occurs is serving your highest good. Believe it.

Fear-Fueled Illusion 2: Loss

This is a tricky one. Loss is something we periodically experience throughout our lives. We lose jobs, friendships, marriages, loved ones. Though there are clearly degrees of loss, they are each very real and set in motion events that we cannot predict, leaving us feeling adrift, grieving, and lost, trying to find our way back to whatever life looks like in the aftermath. We can't predict when it might happen or what form it will take. In this section, we are going to focus on the kind of loss we believe we are setting ourselves up for by taking particular actions or showing up more authentically as ourselves. When it comes to the fear of loss that we are exposing ourselves to, we need a new lens through which to view it, one that keeps us grounded and resisting the urge to breathe into a paper bag at the mere thought of upsetting the apple cart, even if it's precariously balanced to begin with.

The path of self-development is not an easy one. In order to be on the personal development journey, you have recognized that, on some level, life could be better, you could be more *you*, if you took some time to examine your life and make changes that help you align more with who you truly are. For better or worse, when you decide to do that, it can trigger anger, defensiveness, indignation, fear, and even jealousy in those around you. Maybe it's because they perceive the changes as a threat to your relationship, or it may be work they know they need to do themselves and want to avoid. Whatever the reason, know that you CANNOT avoid doing what *you* feel called to do in order to make others more comfortable.

As you work on yourself, you may find that a natural consequence is a feeling of having outgrown certain people or situations. For example, let's say you and your friends like to get together on weekends and decompress. Have a few drinks and shoot the shit. Does the shit-shooting include a lot of complaining? About work? Colleagues? Kids? Spouses? Schedules? You're ready to take it to the next level, but you're surrounded by people who have created a community that thrives on bitching, blaming, and barely surviving. They are likely good people under all that BS, but how they're showing up is in this predominantly unproductive way, focused on what's wrong rather than what's right. Is that really how you want to spend your time? Who you want to hang out with? What you want to attract?

You may drift away from these folks. It can happen naturally, over time, as you choose to spend less time with them and more time with like-minded people, or even alone. If these are people you planned weekends or evenings around, it can be scary to consider what life looks like without them in it, or at least with them in it less frequently. And yes, this is a loss to be processed and grieved, but what it really does is make space in your life for something better. When you are doing the work of self- and life-improvement, you will find that friendships, people, and opportunities that are more aligned to you will come in to fill that space. This does not necessarily hold true when loss happens through your unwillingness to do the uncomfortable personal work. The critical element to keep in mind is that situations that lead to loss are rarely a one-sided deal. You must do the work of self-examination after a loss to determine the role you played and how to make adjustments going forward, or, as we will discuss in Part II of the book, you are doomed to repeat your mistakes until you've learned which adjustments you need to make. Does that sound scary? Good. It's better to learn, mitigate, and grow than to rinse and repeat.

Fear-Fueled Illusion 3: Control

Oh, Control. How desperately we cling to you and convince ourselves that we have you in our grasp. We believe that, above all, we must know how something is going to turn out in order to move forward. We tell ourselves that if we do X and Y, that we will get outcome Z. But does it always work out the way we planned?

Of course not. You can bust your ass and check all the boxes because you think you'll get promoted and then feel blindsided when it doesn't happen. You can pour lessons, time, and money into a child's athletic endeavors, with visions of professional sports dancing in your head, only to have your child quit that sport in pursuit of something else. You can do your best to keep a relationship together, talking openly, seeking counseling, listening to one another, and still that relationship may end. Control is an illusion. It doesn't exist. And the more quickly you come to terms with that, the more rapidly you'll transform your life.

Control is such a double-edged sword. We get a strange sense of comfort in believing it exists, all while being completely oblivious to the fact that the need for control limits us tremendously. Think about it. When you are so completely focused on making something go just the way you want it to, you impose tunnel vision on yourself. Tunnel vision that is focused so completely on one outcome that anything happening simultaneously in the periphery is utterly missed. Simply put, you are not open to opportunity when you're in the grip of the need for control. You've decided what you want, dammit, and even if something better shows up, you won't recognize it. You likely won't even register it.

This is the danger of clinging to control. You are so accustomed to operating in your current framework (which I'll refer to as your "operating framework" going forward) that it's difficult to imagine an opportunity that doesn't look the way you expect it to. One of the most common things I hear when I work with people is that, even though they want more, they can't imagine what that more would be. They say, "Well, all I know is industry A, and I'm pretty much doing the best job available in this industry." Um. No. The idea that you are only qualified to do something that you've already done is severely limiting. Most people have little to no appreciation of how truly talented and skilled they are, and how those talents and skills are transferable to something completely different. If I had ascribed to that way of thinking, I'd be working as a healthcare IT executive somewhere, rather than coaching people and writing this book. And I would still be miserable.

Let go of your iron grip. See the possibilities around you. Be open to the fact that there is indeed something that will light you up and energize you, even if you don't know what it is yet. In fact, if that's where you are as you read this, you're exactly where you need to be. There are probably some unicorn-like creatures who are born knowing their purpose, start doing it at age twenty-two, and do it until they retire, loving it throughout. But those people are not the norm. And I would argue that a life rich with varied experiences puts you on an exciting path where the convergence of those experiences can lead you to a place you couldn't have dreamed of if you'd been operating inside your career/industrial framework.

Get really clear on where the need for control is showing up for you. Is it many areas? Predominantly one or two areas? Don't judge yourself, but ask yourself some questions. What exactly am I trying to avoid by controlling this? What do I think will happen if I don't control this? What happens if I stop controlling and start trusting? We will talk much more about how trust and faith play into this overall personal development journey a little later on.

To Don't:

- **Don't hold onto control with an iron grip**; it doesn't really exist and creates a tunnel vision effect that limits your ability to conceive of a bigger, better life.
- **Don't allow the illusion of security to keep you in the safe place of your comfort zone** where change doesn't happen or happens through a sudden (and generally unpleasant) turn of events.
- **Don't let fear of failure keep you from doing something** you know deep down is an important step for you.

Do Instead:

- **Know that failure is opportunity.** It's not the end of the road, but the beginning of a new one. Change your perspective and let it teach and inform you, then feel empowered to move forward armed with that information and experience.
- **Remember that loss** of situations and associations **makes room** for more aligned people, opportunities, and experiences to come in.
- **Loosen your grip. Control doesn't exist** and it doesn't serve you to continue believing that it does. It limits your ability to see what's possible.

Summing Up

Fear is the layer beneath stagnation and resistance to change. It also serves a purpose, so don't run when it shows up. Now that you have a solid understanding of fear and the various ways it can hold you back and keep you stuck, it's time to start paying close attention to how it's showing up for you personally. When you're taking this inventory, dig deep. Get curious and question yourself to gain a real understanding of the complexity of programming, patterns, and messaging that need to be addressed as you move forward. Remember, you don't have to have the answers right now. You just have to be willing to answer the questions that will allow the answers to come. Be compassionate with yourself and suspend judgment.

It will take some work on your part to gain clarity about the role fear is playing in keeping you small and safe. Get out your journal or have your voice memo phone app handy, and answer the following questions:

1. When does fear tend to show up for me?
2. What is my typical response to fear?
3. When have I done something despite the presence of fear? What was the outcome of acting with courage?
4. When did I experience an outcome that was different than I had planned? How did my lack of control/perception of loss/understanding of failure shift when reviewing that experience in hindsight? What were the positives? Would it have actually served me for it to have turned out how I'd intended?
5. What one area that feels the least scary can I choose to exercise acting in the face of fear? What is the fear, and what would that action look like?

6. What's the worst that could happen if I do the scary thing? For example, if you tend to fear rejection and the worst that could happen is that someone says no to you, how bad is that really? Be willing to look at the worst-case scenario in order to defuse its power.

When fear shows up, thank it for looking out for you. Let fear know you've got this, and have the courage to act anyway.

CHAPTER 6

Don't Just Pray. Row the Damn Boat.

In the last twelve to eighteen months of my career, some serious shit was hitting the fan. I didn't have much peace of mind in that final stretch, even though I had begun a new role I was super excited about. I went on a previously planned vacation right after my first official day in the role, and it was a particularly rough time to be away. Planning for the following year had just begun, and due to my limited familiarity with the new areas of responsibility at that point, I spent most of my vacation on my laptop. I had some vague alarm bells going off in my head about that, because, deep down, I knew without a doubt the can't-get-away laptop lifestyle didn't excite me. I rationalized that because I was new to my role and the timing was bad, so it was a compromise I had to make at that time. Once it all settled down, I wouldn't allow myself to be that person who couldn't take a break from work.

Of course, it quickly became the norm to check in with emails several times a night and over the weekend. I made a deliberate decision to keep separate work and personal mobile phones. I wanted to turn off my work phone sometimes and not see the constant barrage of messages that would otherwise serve as nonstop distractions to living life outside of work. It worked out pretty well, until one weekend my work phone acted up, and a message sent to me on a Sunday didn't actually register on my phone until Tuesday. And, oh lord, the shit storm that ensued.

I traveled that week and had a rather long trip that required a plane change, so my phone stayed off for most of the day. When I arrived at my destination, I finally saw the message that had been left a couple of days before, along with another voicemail and some emails related to the voicemails I had received. I won't go into the boring details, but the gist is that a project I had had zero involvement with needed to have some adjustments and be resubmitted, and the deadline to do so was that day. My initial reaction was to panic. How the eff had I missed those initial messages?? And what the eff was this project, and how had it become my responsibility??

With an underlying unease (that I was trying to keep from escalating into panic) as my constant companion, I spent the day on the phone with various people, trying to quickly learn what I needed to so I could write long emails with justifications for the changes requested, only to be told by the requester that my reasoning didn't measure up and what about angles A, B, and C? I ended up missing the event I had traveled for in its entirety, my day consumed by this pseudo-emergency that could easily have waited until the person who actually had the details became available. But no. Urgency and reactivity were so much a part of the culture that they had to be manufactured even if they didn't exist. I got swept up into the bullshit and, for the first time in my career, wondered seriously if I would be fired for what had transpired, even though my state of confusion about how I had ended up responsible for the mess persisted.

This incident was a major turning point for me. It was one of the most miserable experiences of my career. I felt completely disempowered, at the mercy of outside events, and very clear about the extent to which I was devalued as an associate and, worse yet, as a person. My track record and accomplishments meant nothing. That I was competent and dedicated meant nothing. In that moment, the only thing that mattered was this one thing, and until I resolved it, nothing that came before it mattered at all. It didn't enter into the equation that I should be treated as a human being. As a resource, it was up to me to get shit done yesterday. I had no background on the subject and was out of town for a client event, but no one cared. It was some seriously *Twilight Zone* shit. And I'm really glad it went down the way it did.

I absolutely needed to see that I didn't matter as a cog in the machine I was part of. If told to jump, the only response was to ask how high, thank you, and don't you worry your pretty head about what time of day or night it is, whether or not you have the details, just do as you're told. Fuck. All. Of. That. I knew right then and there that I couldn't spend the rest of my career in an environment like that.

I could have decided that I was a victim. Poor me, they were so mean, why were they always trying to make my life harder? I could have put my head down, let the life force seep out of me, and become a robot in pursuit of being a good soldier, so I could keep getting that fat salary and awesome benefits. But what the incident showed me in no uncertain terms was that I can't hang in a situation like that. I didn't let my dad beat the spirit out of me, and I sure as hell wouldn't allow my job to do so. I could have continued to commiserate with other super bright and capable people, all of whom had similar stories that we could tell over "happy" hours to make ourselves feel better because we weren't alone in our misery. It was just a fact of corporate life that was to be tolerated, if not celebrated. But staying there, tolerating such behavior, will turn you into a victim, whether you want it to or not. It steals your power when you let people devalue you and accept it as the natural course of things, instead of standing up for yourself and declaring "No more of this shit."

Entirely too much of your life is happening to you without your intervention. You wait to be told what to do, where to turn, which decisions to consider, what's possible—the list goes on. You're living in a state of reactivity, waiting for life to serve something up that you can respond to, rather than acting with intention to create what you really want.

When I decided enough was enough, that was only the beginning. My first thoughts went straight to the typical alternative when we are unhappy in our jobs—where else I could apply. What I was qualified for, what would be less miserable. As I pictured myself in these alternate work universes, I began to realize that

I would still be trapped. A change of scenery wouldn't address the underlying reasons I felt I had for leaving. I had experienced enough role changes in previous years to know that a jolt of energy accompanies change. You are energized to go into the new situation, learn something new, get familiar with new people, and acclimate, only to find, once you've acclimated, that underneath the shiny newness, nothing has really changed. I had this experience within the same company, moving from role to role only to find that, even with a better manager and team, eventually I would settle in and the exact same feelings would return. If you've had this experience and are not careful to be conscious of how you got there, you can slip into assuming you are the problem instead of understanding that the solution lies within you. The only problem at hand is whether or not you'll make the effort to clear out the noise and get to the bottom of what's keeping you down.

Reclaim Your Power

You take yourself with you into the new situation. And *you* are what needs to level up. As a high achiever, you must believe that you have the power to do this for yourself. The fact that high achievers get to the point where they feel as if there's no way out points to just how powerful your programming is. So much so that, despite evidence to the contrary regarding your capabilities, you behave as if life is happening to you instead of taking active steps to create what you want.

We've been talking about work here, but the same holds true for personal relationships. If you are allowing someone else to call the shots and reacting to those calls, you are disempowered in that relationship. There are about ten million ways in which this can show up, so let's call out some examples to get your juices flowing about where in your life this might be showing up:

- "My husband never helps with the dishes. He just sits on the couch after dinner watching TV while I run around cleaning up, even though I'm the one who cooked dinner. We've talked about it before, but he either doesn't remember we've talked about it or he doesn't care. He just keeps doing nothing."

- "My wife never lets me help with anything. I'll ask if I can help, but even if she lets me, she nitpicks about how I'm doing things and makes it so miserable for me that I don't bother to ask anymore. I'll ask if I can help, she'll get annoyed and tell me no, so I just walk away and don't ask anymore. She wants to do it her way and makes me feel like I can't do anything right."
- "My friend Sue is flaky about keeping dates to see each other. When she's having a crisis, she texts and calls and wants to find a time to meet, but then she reschedules more often than not, especially if she's not in crisis mode anymore. Sometimes she "forgets" we were supposed to hang out or doesn't let me know until the last minute. She says she's bad about keeping her calendar organized. I just know and plan for the fact that she's probably going to bail on me."

The one thing each of these scenarios has in common is the disempowered approach taken by the person relating these stories. If you're in a marriage, you're in a partnership, period. If your partner isn't behaving as such, do something about it. In the first scenario, the wife wants her husband to participate in running the household. Initiate a meeting to talk about household duties, sit down together, talk through what makes sense, then post a chore chart if you need to. No excuses for "forgetting" something needs to be done or getting out from under it. If you are the person who avoids helping out because of critical feedback, speak up. Now is the time to let your partner know why you don't help and how it makes you feel to have your way of doing things picked apart. But also, stop asking how you can help and just get up and do what needs to be done. "Help" implies that the responsibility isn't yours and you want to pitch in. Talk to your partner about household responsibilities and divide them up. End of statement. Each person needs to be okay with the other doing things their own way, or you risk getting into a parental/authority figure dynamic which is far from sexy and will damage the rest of your relationship. But above all, STOP walking away with your tail between your legs because someone didn't do what you asked; stop tolerating the status quo if it isn't working for you, and find the shared solution.

These may seem like petty issues to focus on, but when present, they are symptomatic of a larger problem, that of waiting for life to happen to you and resigning yourself to low expectations. You might be thinking to yourself, "But I've tried!" Maybe, but you've never tried with the level of self-awareness you are developing now. If you didn't expect more from life, you wouldn't be reading these words. The challenge is that living according to the expectations of others sets us up to be reactive. We wait for something to happen so we can respond to it. There's very little proactivity. Call to mind the words you hear or think on a regular basis:

"What's meant to happen will happen!"
"I'll wait and see what opportunities come up."
"I guess it wasn't meant to be."
"Let's see what happens next time."

Have you picked up on the common thread here? Where are YOU in these scenarios? Waiting for something to happen. As if you have no say in the matter and can't possibly participate in defining what comes next.

When I was a freshman in high school, I was in an advanced lit class where we read and studied mythology. As if the content and meatiness of stories like *The Iliad* weren't enough inspiration, the teacher had taken the time to post numerous inspirational thoughts around the room and above the blackboard. I'm guessing she hoped that these inspirational thoughts would penetrate our young, impressionable minds. One of those thoughts drew my attention every single day I spent in that class and stuck with me for the rest of my life. The statement was "Pray to God but row to shore."

That's exactly what we are talking about here.

Look for support, for inspiration, pray, think positively, but for the love of all that is right in the world, be proactive about going after what you want. Not doing this is akin to deciding it's time for a relationship, putting a profile on an online dating site, and then sitting back to wait and see who gets in touch with you, when you can and should be out there looking at profiles to see who attracts your interest. How much less engaged can you be? I guess you could be less engaged if you're sitting around hoping for a lover and expecting said lover to run you over with a shopping cart at the grocery store and just happen to be the "one" that is your happily-ever-after. Stop waiting for life to happen to you.

I don't mean to suggest that you should do away with openness to possibilities. Not at all. On the contrary, what I'm saying is that you'll be better at recognizing the most aligned opportunities if they show up after you've done the work of defining what you want. It's much easier to know if an opportunity is one you should pursue when you know what your yes/no column consists of. For example, let's say you're fed up to your eyebrows with your current job and want to find another one. You don't bother to sit down to deeply consider what it is that you like about your job now and what's not working for you; you just decide to look to "see what happens." You get an interview and ultimately an offer with such good money you're over the moon, and you accept. Once you've spent a few months in the new job, the honeymoon period is over and you realize it has too much of what you were trying to get away from—travel, project deadlines, a long commute, etc. You're back to square one, defeated because you thought you had found an escape hatch to greener pastures. By now, you're probably catching on to the fact that there is no escape hatch because you can't jettison yourself from the equation.

I've said this before and I'll say it again—if you don't do the work when the opportunities present themselves, you will repeat some variation of the same patterns, experiences, and emotions you were looking to get away from. The only way out is through, and you'll come out more empowered and with greater clarity about what you want and which steps to take next.

Your programming is of critical importance in this context. What you see/saw your parents and friends do can be subtly but highly influential in the way you process your reality and the extent to which you have power to influence that reality. If, for instance, organized religion was a big part of your upbringing or your way of life now, you may be surrounded by people who believe the answer to any and all problems is to pray. There is nothing wrong with prayer; it can be an effective way to put your struggle into words and be open to asking for assistance. However, it is ineffective if you don't take inspired action on your own behalf. This is the equivalent of praying for a miraculous cure to the cancer inside your body but refusing to look into the treatment options, traditional or not, that exist to help you fight that battle. You must be willing to take up proverbial arms on your own behalf. If *you* don't put forth effort for yourself, why should anyone else?

To Don't:

- **Don't stay in reactive mode.** Waiting and seeing isn't a strategy. Reactivity is a state in which you wait for life to happen to you and determine your next steps based on those events. Living in this manner robs you of dreaming bigger and taking intentional steps to create something different.
- **Don't believe you can positive-think or pray your way out of your situation**. Those are powerful tools, but not the full arsenal. You must act.
- **Don't look externally to explain why your life is where it is.** All that tells you is what you're tolerating and resigning yourself to. You are not a victim of your circumstances unless you choose to be.

Do Instead:

- **Be intentional.** Choose to create what you desire instead of waiting to see what happens next. Step out of reactivity and into deliberate thoughts and actions.
- **Take inspired action.** Pray and think positively if that helps you, but you must take inspired action that moves you closer to what you are attempting to create. The world will respond if you show up; it has no interest in doing so if you aren't engaged in the process.
- **Be empowered.** If you need or want something, articulate it. Go after it.

Summing Up

You have all the power within you to take an assertive approach to going after what you want. A disempowered approach to life, one in which you are the mercy of what's taking place around you, makes you vulnerable to the victim mindset. Refusal to look at your own role in what's happening in your life keeps you in victim mentality, where pointing fingers may give you a sense of righteousness and permission to be wounded, but ultimately does not serve you and only works to keep you stagnant.

Consider the following to assist in gaining clarity on behaviors that you can change to better serve you.

1. Where in your life have you resigned yourself to a state of being that saps your energy? Is it feeling isolated in a partnership where the other person isn't pulling their weight? Do you have a goal you keep trying to reach, but have yet to take all the steps necessary to reach it?
2. When do you look outside of yourself, e.g. slide into victim mindset or the blame game, for justification about where you are in a particular area of your life? Are you looking to assign fault to a person or situation?
3. Once you've identified the areas in which you have a disempowered approach, start asking yourself the following:

    a. Why am I putting up with this?
    b. How do I keep myself from taking the steps I know I should?
    c. How is my current approach affecting my life?
    d. What can I do in each of these situations to take inspired action that will help me move forward?

4. After you come up with your list of ways you can move forward, choose one area to begin with and put your energy toward taking the steps you've identified. Once you've made enough progress, you will naturally feel energized to repeat

the process with the other areas you've identified, so you can add those on as you see fit.

5. Watch for complacency! After you've seen some good results from your efforts, it can be easy to decide you've "done enough" and assume the other areas aren't as important or you'll get to them eventually. All of the work you're doing is like working a muscle to make it stronger and more efficient. The more you do the work, the faster and easier it will become, so don't self-sabotage by slowing your momentum.

CHAPTER 7

The Dangerous Allure of Conditions

Ever tell yourself that the thing you really want to do will get done when the time is right? When some other project is over? When your life gets easier in one of ten ways? Chances are there are underlying, sometimes hidden, reasons you avoid doing the thing you need to do. You tell yourself that the ideal time to do the thing is when a condition or set of conditions is met, enabling you to delay ever getting started, because, let's face it—when are conditions 100 percent favorable for any given endeavor? You and I both know that the answer is rarely, if ever. This pattern of avoidance or delay based on less-than-ideal external conditions is what I will refer to as being conditional or conditionality.

Of all the ways to make excuses, this may be the most dangerous of all. The reasons you give yourself and others sound perfectly reasonable, and much of the time, the roadblocks you throw out are technically true. However, if perfect timing is the impossible standard you've set for getting started on anything that moves you forward in life, you are participating in your own stagnation, big time. There is no such thing as the right time for anything. If you insist on waiting for it, you'll be waiting indefinitely while life continues to pass you by.

It may not be immediately obvious to you the ways in which conditions are interfering with your ability to get moving in your life. Let's look at some of the common ways in which this shows up for people. Keep in mind that conditions can be internal or external, meaning that it can be your own inner landscape that's in your way, or something outside of you that gets in your way.

- Waiting to get started with a weight loss plan until that project at work is over so you can get to the gym.
- Vowing to spend more time with your family when things at work are less hectic.
- Deciding that you'll work on your marriage when your partner finally steps up to participate.
- Promising you'll be a better friend after this initial period of building your business is over.
- Telling yourself that you'll take the time to do some self-care when the kids have fewer activities and your nights and weekends aren't so full of commitments.
- Resolving that your mood will improve once you get the win, after you know how something will be resolved, when your favorite team wins the sporting event, etc.

Does any of this sound familiar? Conditionality is when taking steps toward the outcome you desire is dependent on certain conditions having been met. Why is this so bad? Because no matter what conditions you've settled upon in the moment, something else will come up to derail you. Let's say project A at work is finally wrapping up, so now you can focus on establishing your workout regimen. Sounds great, right? But a couple of days into it, you get word that another project will be starting within the next two weeks, so there's really no point in getting started with those workouts now. You might as well wait until this next project is over. And those plans you had to take a trip with your family will have to change, because there's no way you'll have time to do that once the project begins. It will have to wait.

It will have to wait. Does work wait? Do your professional deadlines wait? When you stop to think about it, what is it that you put on hold? As a high achiever, work takes priority above all, contributing directly to the conditions that make you feel stuck. You're in a loop of doom, where you desperately want more but won't allow yourself to have it.

Before you know it, you've spent a good part of your life creating delays in key areas where lack of action is seriously impacting your well-being, but, because life isn't perfectly poised to help you succeed, you've decided you'll fail, so why even begin? Fear of failure participates in this cycle of delays/avoidance because you can't fail at what you haven't attempted. You can maintain the rose-colored-glasses outlook, where you can keep hope of success alive in a fail-safe way. You allow hope to sustain the status quo rather than taking action to create the change you desire, protecting you from the challenge of doing the work, putting in the effort, and finding that additional work or rework may be necessary to truly create your desired outcome. You may be secretly or subconsciously afraid of failure and therefore avoid the forward motion that could take you there.

When I first started thinking about writing a book, I was hopped-up on conditions for days. Very early on, it was fun and exciting to think about, but part of the fun was a result of how far off it appeared to be at the time. I adore doing research on everything under the sun, so I gleefully got to work on looking into just what it takes to write a book. I read, watched videos, checked out writing coaches, subscribed to blogs, and finally settled upon an online course that covered everything I needed to know about writing a nonfiction book proposal. I was excited to get started. I came up with a plan for how I would fit the course into my schedule and began.

My excitement quickly changed to trepidation. Holy shit, what had I gotten myself into? Why did I think I could do this? Just looking at the accompanying documents made my head hurt, as I couldn't conceive of accomplishing each of the milestones that were a part of drafting a professional, industry-appropriate proposal that would get the attention of a publisher. I didn't give up, but

I definitely dialed back my effort, telling myself that it wasn't the right time to start the book, anyway. At least I had what I needed and could start when the time was right, which wasn't when I was still navigating how to leave my job and establish my new business. I then started in on one of my favorite ways to delay, getting my folders organized and making sure the space on my computer was in tip-top shape for "the right time." Once everything was just so, I walked away with a silly sense of satisfaction for having gotten myself organized for "someday."

I didn't totally walk away from the effort, however. One thing I have going for me is that I generally reject my own attempts at rationalization (because my own excuses make me uncomfortable), so I did make some progress over time. As soon as the step I was working on got more challenging than I was comfortable with, I'd walk away. My coaching business picked up, and then I decided it really wasn't the right time and set aside the proposal for several months.

One day, I received a message through an email subscription about an online summit on the subject of writing a transformational book. Huh, I thought. That's interesting. It was one of those roundabout messages that always get my attention, this time especially because I'd never heard of this summit before, and I wouldn't have known about it if another coach I'd been following hadn't decided to spread the word through her own list. It felt like synchronicity, as if it was a wake-up call I should listen to, at least long enough to see if it was of interest. After looking through the agenda, I decided to sign up. At the very least, I thought, a lot of the information would come in handy when the time was right to get going with the proposal again.

One of the best things about the summit was that it had time-sensitivity built in, which helped create a sense of urgency on my part. Each day had hours and hours of interview content, but replays were only available for forty-eight hours unless you wanted to pay for the upgrade. I didn't want to pay—the timing wasn't right, after all—so I made it a point to check the agenda the day before, noted the content I was most interested in, and watched hours of content that entire week. The very next week, I contacted one of the interviewees about his publication crowdfunding platform. He asked me to send him what I had, which turned out to be much more than I had given myself credit for, and encouraged me to be ready to launch my book proposal five weeks from then. I was far from ready for launch and there was still a lot to do, but having that conversation had flipped a switch in my head. I recognized that everything was pushing me toward now rather than later, and I'm one to pay attention to signs and synchronicities when they show up. I did the remaining work, launched as we had discussed, and you know how it turned out because you're reading these words.

Now or Later?

We tend to ascribe mystery to timing, as if "right timing" has some magically perfect element that launches us to heights of success, and without it we are doomed to fail. Of course, there are periods in our lives where it's not ideal to pursue a new adventure due to the kind of energy and focus it will require; however, those periods are actually much fewer and farther between than we are willing to admit. Most of the time, you can decide that now is what's available to you, so now is the time. If the excuse that pops up for you is that there isn't enough time, dial back your expectations. Instead of committing to go to the gym five days a week, tell yourself you're going to start now and go two or three days a week and will work your way up from there. If you want to work on your relationship but your partner is resistant to the idea that there's anything to work on, start working on yourself. Read, go to a therapist, journal, determine what you can do on your own and commit to doing it. Your partner may come along or may not. Either way, you need to know, right? Don't let conditions that create dependency on others dictate what you will or won't do.

We are surrounded by people who operate this way, which makes it even trickier for us as individuals to shut out this kind of messaging and stop making excuses for delaying what we know we need to do. In case you haven't noticed, delaying isn't the same thing as dismissing. The only thing delay accomplishes is making sure that whatever that thing is, it's going to take up a ton of space in your head, maybe even permanent residence, if you don't just do it already. Chances are, the more it hangs out there, the more its friends guilt and shame will show up to the party, exponentially increasing how not-awesome you feel about avoiding what needs to be done. Doesn't feel good, does it? GOOD. That's the whole point. The crappy feelings are there to help spur you forward, to take action so the crappiness goes away. It's like a built-in remedy that exists for your benefit. Don't want to do this thing now? Fine. We'll wait. And make you feel shitty about it. Until the shitty feelings make you get off your ass because you're sick of the shit. Yay! Mission accomplished. But seriously, why does it have to be that way? Why can't you just decide to move forward?

Identify Avoidance

Waiting for the conditions to be perfectly lined up is a non-plan. Thinking in such a way is a habit that must be broken. It's simply a self-propagating pattern, a feedback loop that continues until you've decided not to participate. As silly as it may sound, coming up with affirmations that negate what you generally tell yourself about conditions and repeating them over time establishes a new habit while it breaks the old one. Sit down and think about all the times you say to yourself:

"I will ________ when ________."

Going back to my example, my message to myself was, "I will write a book when it's time." Talk about vague and useless. When is "it's time?" I could let that go on forever, it's so poorly defined and without boundaries. For you, maybe it's, "I'll start eating right when I'm traveling less." Well, okay. But when will you travel less? Is travel an integral part of your job? Just how long will this travel be a regular part of your life? The conditions we impose are often about our interactions with others, as well. Is there a conversation you know you need to have with someone but it won't be easy, so you're putting it off? Maybe you tell yourself, "I'll talk to him about that the next time we meet in person." Why don't you make the arrangements to meet in person, then? Is this someone who you rarely see in person, so that condition helps you further delay what needs to be said?

Conditionality is an avoidance tactic. There are certainly times when it makes sense to consider conditions before making your move, particularly if the situation in question involves your relationship with another. For instance, calling up your friend to have it out with him when you know he lives in the path of the hurricane that's bearing down on his home isn't the right move. The conditions are far from ideal—they are nowhere near appropriate. In this case, waiting until your friend is on the other side of this event and doing okay is the best move. Well, yeah. You might be thinking this is an extreme and somewhat silly example. Who would do that? Take a moment to consider whether you've ever had a conversation when the timing really was inappropriate and how it turned out. The danger of conditional action is that it can lull you into a simmering state, one in which you've delayed a necessary conversation for so long that you essentially blow your lid at the wrong time, potentially making the situation worse because now emotions are high and you're having it out instead of having a conversation. What was the point of waiting?

Embrace Imperfection

Hidden beneath operating conditionally is the subtlety of perfectionism. It's as if there's only one right way to do what you're waiting to do, so until it's possible to do it in that one perfect way, there's no point in trying. Take the "I'll eat better when I travel less" example. You can make better choices now, can't you? Or is the real issue that you must follow some dietary guidelines 100 percent of the time in order to feel like you're doing it "the right way?" The same is true of health and exercise regimens. What is the point of delaying until you have the time to work out six days a week? Will your body not benefit from three days if you get started now? Are you not ready to apply for that job because you believe you need three more certifications in order to be truly competitive? How do you know, and what's the harm in applying? Do not allow the perfect to be the enemy of the good. The same is true if your tendency is to quit at something because you can't do it the way you should be doing it. Says who? What is all this *should* nonsense? Do it in the way that works for you, period. That's the only right way there is, the only way you'll make progress and stick with anything you attempt long enough to see the benefits.

Conditionality is a major factor in how you operate when you don't appropriately prioritize your life. When everything has equal weight, you run around like a chicken with its head cut off, trying to cram everything in because you haven't taken the time to weigh which of the things on your list are more important. For example, let's say you've been delaying taking a course and certification exam that's going to help your chances of getting a promotion. It won't take long once you've committed, but there are always reasons to delay. You don't have enough time because of the kids' activities, your project at work is taking all of your focus, you caught a virus and had to recover, etc. The excuses here are all related to a lack of time. Now, the question is, does this promotion align with your priorities and your new definition of success? You're not sure, so now you know the first step you must take is determining whether this promotion is something you truly want. Have you been told it's the next step in your career? Are you concerned it means you are lazy and a loser if you're okay with staying where you are? Have you been avoiding the larger question, which is, does your current career light you up in a way that inspires you to continue to grow, or is it time to look at other options? Get clarity, prioritize based on what you know, and decide to either proceed with or let go of this particular thing that's hanging out, sucking up the energy you could be putting toward making real progress.

When it comes to your state of mind, conditionality is an excuse for staying in an emotional or mental rut that is ultimately disempowering and puts you in the position of dependency on external conditions to improve what's happening with you internally. One afternoon, I had a meeting with a woman I'd become acquainted with through a series of speaking engagements I had presented through a local professional networking organization. She had recently left her career to become a consultant, eager to create wealth in her life rather than settling for just a paycheck. At this point, it was very early in her entrepreneurial endeavor and, as is so common in the beginning, she was riding the waves that would crest in excitement and inspiration, then trough in fear of failure and the unknown. As we talked through how it was going over a glass of wine, she said, "I know I'll feel better when I get a win." I responded with, "When you feel better, you'll get a win."

She raised her eyebrows, widened her eyes, sat back in her chair, and said "You know what, that makes total sense to me. I have to get in the right frame of mind or the win won't come." BINGO.

When you focus on conditions and how they fall short of the ideal, it creates a pattern in which you spend a lot of energy on how the conditions fall short and how you can change them, rather than affirming what you desire in a way that flips the switch in your head from disempowered to empowered.

Disempowered: "I'll feel better when I get a win." Whether this win is in the form of a promotion, job offer, contract, etc., it's all the same. You abdicate responsibility for your happiness and for the win to outside forces, as you are at the mercy of not having the win and therefore feeling less than great about the situation, essentially keeping yourself trapped there.

Empowered: "I'm going to get that win. I'm confident it's coming, so I'm going to keep doing what I'm doing in excited anticipation of its arrival." You've flipped from the passive state of waiting for the win to determination to make it happen, staying confidently engaged in the process and looking forward to celebrating it once it occurs. You can further sweeten this approach by thinking about just how you'll celebrate and starting to look forward to it now. A subtle shift can flip your perspective and take you from the passenger seat to the driver's seat in an instant.

To Don't:

- **Don't use the conditions that surround you as an excuse for stagnation.** Waiting for the "right" timing or environment becomes a chronic mode of operation; as one set of conditions exits, another will come in to take its place and provide a continuation of reasons to delay.
- **Don't allow your mental state to be dictated by what's happening around you**. Doing so makes you a passive bystander who is waiting for X to occur so you can feel Y.
- **Don't tell yourself what you "should" be doing.** Conditions can be used as a way of blocking progress toward something you don't really want. If, for instance, you've been delaying taking steps toward getting the promotion that's been on your mind, take a beat and ask yourself if you truly want the promotion or if it's something you're supposed to want or that others are telling you is the next logical step.

Do Instead:

- **Flip your perspective, be confident about the direction you are moving in**, and create the mental and emotional environment in which **good things can happen because you expect them to.**
- **Identify the ways in which you are allowing conditions to dictate how you feel and what you do.** The conditions you use as excuses aren't going to change anytime soon, so while they provide you with good cover from having to move forward, inaction invites guilt and shame to the party, piling on and making it more and more uncomfortable to remain in place.
- **Get clear on what you want**. Drop all the "I should" thoughts around actions and contemplate what it is you wish to do. Go back and review your thoughts regarding your definition of success and make sure this thing hanging over your head is in line with that definition, and, if it's not, let it go.

Summing Up

Allowing conditions to dictate when and how you take action and how you feel is a dangerous way to keep yourself exactly where you are. Once you identify the ways in which conditions you've defined keep you in place, you will be empowered to watch for excuses, observe when you are unconsciously striving for perfection or hinging your mood on dependencies, and remind yourself that there's no magical right time that will contribute to massive change and instant success in one fell swoop. The reality of life is that we make progress toward our goals and dreams, rather than achieving them instantly through strokes of good fortune or luck. The less conditionally you operate, the more strides you'll make, and the more quickly and efficiently *you* will create what you desire. The more you keep your head up, keep going, and expect the best, the more likely it is that you will manifest what you want. You have all the power. Act as if you do, stop waiting, quit wallowing, and get started. There is no right time. There is only now.

Time to get clear on how conditions are hindering forward movement in your life.

1. When do you use conditions as an excuse for not moving forward? To get you started, consider the following areas and see if you can identify patterns of conditionality in any of them: physical health, work projects, relationships, self-care, leisure time, daily routines, etc.
2. When do you allow your state of mind to depend on what's happening around you? What can you say to yourself that flips your perspective from passive conditionality to empowered and confident expectation of the desired outcome?
3. Identify any themes that pop up. Is lack of time a common excuse? Are you attempting to avoid perceived difficulty, whether it's in relation to others or about you specifically? Is fear of failure buried beneath your conditions, so not starting protects you from failing?
4. Is a drive for perfection keeping you locked in place? Do you feel there are set parameters around "the right way"

and there's no point in getting started if you can't make it perfect from the get-go? What are you telling yourself in areas where you are particularly stagnant due to this need for perfection?

5. Determine what small steps you can take to move forward. Drop the need for perfection, acknowledge the excuses, review your priorities, and come up with one to three steps you can take to break the stagnation.

PART III

SYSTEM UPDATE

CHAPTER 8

What Are You Worth?

When I first started to question whether to stay on my career path, money was one of the very first considerations to pop into my head. I mean, I was doing *so* well. Making more money than I had even dreamed possible when I was young and projecting what felt like a big salary, only to be totally blown away by the one I was actually bringing in at that point in my career. I won't lie to you and tell you that I dismissed the thought as unimportant. On the contrary, I knew just how important it was. My drive to achieve was in no small part fueled by the tangibility of financial success.

What had gained equal importance was what I was tolerating to make that salary in the particular way that I was making it.

In my coaching experience, both formal and informal, it's nearly inevitable that the very first "but" in the discussion about finding out what really lights someone up is "But I can't make less money. And there's no money (or some variation thereof) in what I really want to do."

Of all the reasons people use to not do what they really want to do, this one pisses me off the most. I'm not pissed at the person, but at the bullshit programming around "realistic" expectations that creates that kind of thinking in the first place.

Since we are far enough into the process to do a little breakdown, let's look at the ways in which this rationalization of there being no money in whatever lights you up is holding you back:

- It stops you cold before you can even start. Before you've even taken one step, you've slammed the door shut on whatever it is that lights you up, or might, if you gave it half a chance. There's no money. Do not pass go. Do not collect $200. Go straight to—or remain in—jail.
- It comes fully stocked with the two most insidious and damaging limiting beliefs: **There is not enough** (money in this idea, people who want this, market opportunity, etc.) and **I am not enough** (not smart enough, not talented enough, not driven enough, etc.).
- It reeks of fear. Because of all of the above. There's no money in it, it's a dumb idea, and I'm not smart enough to make it happen.
- It's all-or-nothing thinking. Who says you have to quit your job to try your hand at whatever it is you're contemplating? There are ways to proceed that have nothing to do with ditching your career and your salary when it feels totally unsafe to do so.
- It is dismissive. Of you, your talent, the value you can bring. And perhaps most of all, it's dismissive of the people out there who want this thing you have inside of you, only they don't even know they want it because you won't act on it.

If all of that isn't enough to make you stop and think, consider this. When you refuse to truly consider the possibilities that pop up for you, likely repeatedly, you have decided to stay in a compromise that isn't working for you. That consists of continuing to trade your time, health, peace of mind, and overall fulfillment for a salary.

I get that it's not all about the money. It's about what that money has provided for you in terms of lifestyle. You can buy nice clothes, the best cars, live in a great neighborhood, go on 1.5 vacations a year and stay in nice hotels, get your nails done, play golf. Or maybe not. Are you even doing any of these things for yourself? Are you so steeped in scarcity that paying a little money for some self-indulgence feels like excess to you? Do you bargain-shop, do your own nails, stay at home and watch TV instead of playing a sport because all those things cost money?

Even if you are indulging in fabulous activities and making small investments in yourself, they cannot fill the "Is this all there is?" hole that's hanging out in your mind and heart, creating negative space that yearns to be filled. If you are hanging your hat on the fact that you do indeed take time off and spend some money here and there, the bar for your life is too low.

It's critical to revisit your programming with the particular question of "What are you worth?" at the center of your thought process. What were you taught about your value?

I didn't have much going for me in this department. As a child, I was left alone a lot. I had a father who told me repeatedly in various ways, verbally and through his actions, that I wasn't worth anything. When I complained that I had too many responsibilities for a child my age, caring for my much younger siblings and being expected to clean the house every day before my parents arrived home, my father would say to me, "You're the maid around here and nothing more." If I was struggling with homework and couldn't answer something correctly, he would take me to the basement and whack me on the backs of my hands with a yardstick. If I talked back, I would be, at best, ignored, or at worst, beaten. I learned to fly under the radar. Do as I was told, stay out of the way, not ask questions, and be on the lookout for signs that the atmosphere was ripe for conflict, doing whatever I could to avoid a blow-up. It was much too complicated for me to grasp with any complexity at that age, but essentially, I was taught that I was a trigger for conflict if I showed up in any visible, challenging way.

My parents both worked my entire life and made enough money for us to live a solidly lower-middle-class life, but I watched my father's misery with more and more awareness as I matured. As an adult, I can see that my father's rage was the result of his terrible self-loathing. I didn't recognize the cycle of abuse for what it was when I was a child, but sometimes there was a period of remorse following an episode of abuse (typically physical—he didn't seem to register verbal abuse as something to be sorry for) during which he would write. My mother would come across his writing and share with me how tortured he was about something he'd done, to the point where he called himself names and questioned the point of his existence. I believe she shared these writings with me to excuse his behavior ("See? Dad is sorry, but next time you shouldn't provoke him."), but they revealed a deep lack of self-worth that could have easily infected me and disrupted the course of my life if I hadn't remained almost militantly self-aware as a preventive to turning out like my father.

My father's lack of belief in himself was nearly breathtaking. When I was born, he was working on his PhD in psychology. He took all the classes, did all the work, wrote his dissertation, and simply never finished it. I've never asked him about it. Never asked him why he made that choice. I didn't feel the need to ask when I was old enough to think of doing so. It was plain to see that he was overflowing with some toxic stew of limiting beliefs that didn't allow him to break through that barrier. From my perspective, he felt unworthy of the accomplishment. And perhaps there was a touch of rebellion in there, too. He had gone to live with his grandmother at the age of fourteen, when the tension between him and his own father reached a tipping point and they could no longer coexist in the same space. On some level, maybe there was some tension around achieving the outcome that would have met his father's expectations, and that was just enough reason not to do it. On another level, his father's lack of belief in him may have created the void of self-worth that I witnessed, and he simply wasn't able to overcome it.

He went from not completing his PhD to taking a punishing role as a juvenile detention officer in a center that was fifty miles from our home. He worked nights and was rarely around for most of my waking hours. I don't remember much about that time, as I was only six years old, but I do remember the day he came home, his face distorted and bruised and ribs broken from a terrible beating he took from some kids who managed to sneak the keys and get out of their rooms with sinister plans. He left that job not long after, but it's no coincidence that, after he earned his Master of Library Science degree, he chose to work in the state prison system. My dad literally chose jail as the place to spend decades of his life. He didn't believe he was worthy of anything better than that.

The persistence of my father's sense of unworthiness, combined with our interactions throughout my childhood, set up a strange emotional juxtaposition between fears that I wasn't worth much and the knowledge that I had intrinsic value. I was lucky to have that sense of myself; the mystical part of me believes it was protection from the angels, this refusal to believe what my father said to me and what his own father likely had said to him. But, as is often the case, the fear-based part of our psyches tends to win the battle when it comes to the unknown territory of stepping outside our comfort zones to create a different experience. That's when the fear-driven part of you wants to chime in with, "You aren't good enough to pull that off." And unfortunately, it's during just those times when we are most vulnerable to that message.

If there's a part of you that's piping up with "Wait, what if my childhood was pretty great? Does that mean that none of this applies to me?" Most certainly, no, it doesn't mean that. At all.

You may have had what many people would consider a normal childhood, but that doesn't provide protection from an inaccurate assessment of your worth. Let's look at a few examples to get your wheels turning about what subtle messages may have been buried in all the normal you experienced.

Normal childhood experience A: My mom stayed home with us kids and my dad worked in the same job for thirty years until he retired. They're still married!

Sounds idyllic, right? Actually, it sounds a little like the 1950s called and they want their Cleaver family back. There is absolutely nothing wrong with this scenario, so please don't take this the wrong way. But if this is what you're holding up as the reason why you have no issues in this department, it's time to take a deeper look.

Was your mom happy at home with her kids? How do you know? Did you ask her? Were you paying attention? Maybe she truly was happy at home, but maybe there was also a little part of her that wished for something different. She made a choice (did she see it that way?) that served your family well, but how well did it truly serve her, and if it did for a while, did it for the duration? What did she give up to do that? How did it impact the way she felt about herself and her contribution? Did she throw herself into all things mother- and wife-related, leaving herself as the last priority?

How did your dad feel about his job? Did he love it? Or did he have to do it because his wife stayed home, and he had kids, and oh by the way, it's what his dad and grandfather did before him so it's just what you do, etc.? Did he do it because that's what men do? Did he have buried dreams, something he would have truly loved to do if he believed he had a choice in the matter? Does he encourage you to be like him, because that's what you do, or does he encourage you to chase your dreams, because that's what he wants you to do instead and wishes he had?

Regarding their still-married status, are they together because their relationship is solid and represents everything you hope to have in your own, or have they made huge compromises to stay married because that's what you do? Do they seem to enjoy each other? Speak respectfully to one another? Are they connected? Did you see things that made you question why they stayed together, and do you see similar themes in your relationship now but stay in it because that's what your parents did?

Normal childhood experience B: I was raised by a single mom. She was amazing. She worked two jobs to make sure we had everything we needed. I look up to her and respect her more than anyone else in the world.

Your mom is amazing, there's no doubt about it. Anyone who manages to raise a child on his/her own is a force of nature. But did you also learn that you must sacrifice yourself for others? That rest and self-care are luxuries rather than necessities? That you should expect to be let down in a relationship? Do you even want a relationship? How did your mother's experience influence your view of what a relationship looks and feels like? What a family looks like? How it impacts your life to have children?

Normal childhood experience C: My mom/dad has an illustrious career. His/her commitment to higher education, along with a passion for his/her work, led to accomplishments that are amazing to behold. He/she is admired and respected by so many. I hope to achieve the same someday.

Why do you hope to achieve it? If you don't, does that mean you should have worked harder? That you're not smart enough? Did you yearn to be an artist, but instead became [insert illustrious profession here] because money and prestige won the battle over creativity?

I could go on and on here, but I think you get the point. No matter how amazingly amazing you think some aspect of your life is, it has programmed you to believe what you believe, and in this chapter in particular, we are talking about the impact these experiences have had on your sense of self-worth. I've said it before, and I'll say it here again: THERE IS NOTHING WRONG WITH THAT! You are who you are because you had all of these experiences, and if I didn't believe that you're awesome and we all need you to show up, I wouldn't bother trying to get you to see what may be hiding in some of your experiences. Awareness is step zero. Without it, you can't do any of the work, because you won't know what you're working on. Embrace it and let's keep going.

Now that we've taken a look at some potential sources of early life programming around what determines worthiness, let's look at your current state and see how this might be showing up for you right now.

Self-Prioritization

One thing a lot of us high achievers have in common is an inability to put our own needs first. Part of what drives us is the need to prove ourselves, so naturally, the tangible proving activities take priority. For me, this was absolutely the case. I would go weeks and weeks with a ridiculously inadequate amount of sleep, and then take pride in how much I was getting done despite my sleep deprivation. When people asked if I was getting adequate sleep (this is how ridiculous it really was—it was like I had achieved a twisted kind of notoriety in being this machine who kept achieving despite running on fumes), I would scoff and flippantly say something really brilliant like, "I'll sleep when I'm dead!" Like it was a badge of honor to be walking around like the living dead.

One of the truly disappointing things about our society and collective programming is that we do often take pride in things that actually hurt us. How often do you hear someone talk about how busy they are like it's something to strive for? Too busy to eat? Skipped lunch? Great! You're such a hard worker. Good on you for not wasting your time on that totally necessary meal that you desperately need because it's literally the only thing you're going to do for yourself all day to allow you to keep going. Never get a massage? That's the right choice. Why waste money on trying to correct your abysmal posture and back pain? You might as well adapt to the comma shape you are morphing into because it will make it that much easier to stay hunched over your laptop.

It's completely bananas, the things we talk about, as if we are in a race to see who can sink to the bottom the fastest. There is nothing good about ignoring your needs, whether they be physical, mental, emotional, or spiritual. It all matters, and if you happen to be overlooking every category listed, it's time to get clear on how disregarding these needs is affecting you. You are sending a very clear message to yourself about your value when you don't make the time or money investment to refill your proverbial tank. So why aren't you doing it?

The most common excuse for not making you a priority?

"I don't have time."

Let's get very clear about what this excuse actually means. What it means is that you don't have *priorities*. You are likely operating in a manner in which everything you think needs to be accomplished carries the same weight, so you must do it all. Here's a quick reminder of the definition of priority for clarity:

> **pri-or-i-ty** (*noun*): a thing that is regarded as more important than another

When you say you don't have time, you're outing yourself as someone who hasn't consciously and thoughtfully gone through the act of prioritizing what in your life makes the most-important list, and you sure as hell aren't on it if it doesn't even exist (if only in your own mind). I guarantee you that not everything on your daily to-do list will make the cut, but you're trying to cram it all in anyway, hence you are "busy" and "overwhelmed" and don't have time for what really matters, like exercise, eating right, bonding with your family, etc.

I had a big wake-up call about priorities when I was in the process of determining how I was going to leave my corporate job. Many months before I left, a woman I knew through a friend contacted me about attending a couples' retreat she would be hosting in a few weeks. Through conversation with my friend, she knew where I was in my exploration of what might come next for me. The retreat was tailored for women who were thinking about a purpose-driven line of work and included their partners so that all could be on the same journey with respect to the mindset and considerations of making such a move. It sounded like exactly what my husband and I needed. I asked her when the retreat would take place. When she told me, I was disappointed to realize that a client meeting I was hosting overlapped with the retreat. I told her it was unlikely I would be able to attend and then proceeded to mope around, feeling defeated by the carrot-dangle of this seemingly perfect opportunity to get serious about doing something different, only to realize that timing was not my friend.

Then I had a realization: my priorities were out of whack.

Here I was, with this golden opportunity to get on the path I'd been thinking about for so long, and I was making my current situation more important than where I wanted to go. Once it became clear to me that my priorities were out of order, it empowered me to think through how I could meet my professional commitment and still make time for creating my path to a different life. I found the solution and was able to attend both. It was a simple matter of getting clear on which opportunity put me first and then deciding that was what needed to happen. As I look back on that decision, it was a clear turning point for me. From that point forward, when faced with a choice about what needs to take priority, I know what to assess and how to confidently decide which is the right choice in the moment.

It may not be comfortable the first few times you boldly put yourself first in the list of considerations, but it will become easier when you realize that choice serves not only you, but also everyone around you. When you're taking care of your own needs, you are putting on your oxygen mask before you assist others. You are more fully present and energized for everyone else in your life. You won't accomplish much more than staggering survival if you insist on continuing to operate on fumes, like a car with a perpetual low fuel light on. Fill your tank, then pile everyone in and zip around getting the important stuff done.

Are you Worthy of the Spend?

Let's go back to the question of whether you even bother to spend money on yourself. Have you made a habit of telling yourself "Well, I don't really *need* that" and talking yourself out of whatever it was that you considered buying?

This may seem like a trivial area to think about, but I'll tell you right now, if you don't believe you are worthy of a little spend unless it's necessary, this is a serious issue and one that must be addressed immediately. I'm not referring to frivolous or compulsive spending that's driven by a desire to fill a void (that, of course, must also be addressed), but rather not spending just because you've learned that spending money on yourself is not a thing that needs to happen.

I had the opportunity to work with one of my favorite people not long after I embarked on my coaching career. She grew up without much parental attention and there was no excess of money. She would say, "I had what I needed" to describe her socioeconomic status as a child. As we started to dig into what her relationship with money was like, it became clear that spending money on herself was a last resort, a thing driven by necessity, which is not at all surprising given her childhood programming. As a respected career professional, she was in a position that required a lot of face time with clients, and therefore her appearance when she showed up for meetings was important. Professional dress was called for, and she absolutely looked the part. But there were times when she'd walk around in a pair of shoes until the soles literally came apart on her walk through the airport, necessitating an emergency trip to buy another pair of goes-with-everything-shoes that would again be worn until they also reached a dire state of wear. Why didn't she have more than one pair of this kind of shoe? Why didn't she feel it was okay to buy a new pair before the old pair disintegrated?

What it came down to was a utilitarian mindset about money. It could only be spent if needed—desire didn't enter the equation. This concept was a bit mind-blowing for me; as a certifiable shoe whore, I felt that I could buy a pair in every color of the rainbow and still covet more. And yet, though she was someone with disposable income, she lived as if in survival mode, being very careful not to spend unless it couldn't be avoided. Her childhood programming was intact and in full operation. It didn't matter that her reality was a major departure from that experience.

There is complexity around our thoughts and feelings about money. We are influenced by what we experienced in our own homes growing up, and beyond that, we are susceptible to ancestral pain in our histories (relatives who survived times of economic hardship) and collective thinking about the economy, its health, and the way that impacts whether we should save or spend.

I have loved clothes and fashion for as long as I can remember. One of my greatest pain points growing up was not having the funds to dress the way I really wanted to. Of course, I grew up during a peak of material flouting when, if you weren't wearing Guess jeans or Reebok high-tops, you might as well hide in the coat closet until the school year was over. I still remember the vivid dreams I had frequently throughout childhood and adolescence about having a closet full of brightly colored, beautiful clothing, with so many options that getting dressed was challenging. I dreamed about it, people. My craving for an amazing wardrobe is something that has stuck with me. I've come to accept it as part of who I am, this desire to create beauty through personal grooming.

I had few options as a kid. I was stuck with the budget my family could afford, and with a mom who was the ultimate bargain shopper ("I looked for hours and found this shirt—only five dollars!!"), there was zero opportunity to fulfill my childhood dreams of the wardrobe stuffed with the latest styles. When I started working in high school, I finally had a little money of my own and would occasionally indulge in spending on a piece of clothing I really wanted, even if I didn't need it. I would leave my shopping bags in the car until a time when I could bring them in unseen. I knew my mom would give me grief about spending too much on things "you don't need" and I didn't want to hear it. We just weren't of the same mind on this subject, and I was going to enjoy myself a little, whether she approved or not.

Hiding in this way set me up to feel shame about caring how I looked and what I wore. When I started college, I was pleasantly surprised (and a little uneasy) to find that getting credit cards was the easiest thing in the world. Plastic broadened my ability to spend, and spend I did. Still mostly in hiding, so now I was up to two no-good things: spending on clothes and racking up debt to do so. It wasn't until I was in my thirties that I was able to truly leave behind the shame I felt about the desire to be surrounded by beauty in all its forms. I appreciate that desire as a valid one, and during that journey, examination of the programming that led me to a place of shame was critical to replacing the old ways of thinking about what I was worthy of.

One particularly vivid memory I have is of a pink and white dress that I adored. It was one of the few clothing items I had that measured up to my standards for what was pleasing, and I wore it a lot. A little drop-waist dress with a pleated skirt. I don't remember exactly how old I was, between seven and nine, but I do remember that I had done something to displease my father, and the consequence was that he cut my little pink and white dress into pieces. Oh, the grief I felt. All I could grasp at the time was that my most favorite dress had been destroyed because I had misbehaved in some way. When I was older, in high school, a fight with my father led to him destroying my makeup. He threw my glass bottle of foundation at the wall and it shattered, leaving a blotch of color with trails oozing down the wall in its wake. Again, tools I used to create beauty were destroyed because I had done something wrong. Are you picking up on the repeated theme here? Shame.

Guilt and shame are at the heart of our worthiness issues. When our sense of self-worth is low, feelings of guilt or shame for who we are in some fundamental way are at play. It's imperative that you wake the fuck up and look at the role guilt and shame are playing in your life, keeping you stagnant, keeping you from loving yourself. The lines of BS you've been fed by others, in terms of their actions or words, must be defused for you to come to an understanding that you're good enough, even when—or *especially* when—others act in ways that make you question yourself.

Money can play an overt or covert role in your sense of self-worth. For me, it was a bit of both. When I was young, I didn't necessarily recognize the direct connection between the creation of beauty and the monetary investment it took to have it. I knew there wasn't enough money to have what I wanted. Later, when I did have enough money to buy what I wanted, I felt ashamed for wanting it. The money question became central to my desire for just about anything—was it worth the investment? When it came to things that had no tangible value, like getting a massage or having a spa day, the real question became, "Am I worth the investment?" The only outcome of such spending is intangible. Relaxation, a little indulgence in luxury, taking the time to nurture myself. Sadly, the majority of the time, my answer was no, I wasn't worth it. How often are you drawing the same conclusion about investing in yourself in small and big ways?

There are many fantastic books on the subject of money mindset, so I will stick with the most important considerations from the standpoint of familiarity with the rut you may be in now. Do you have particular resistance to spending on yourself? Do you talk yourself out of buying new items for your wardrobe, spending on a hobby, treating yourself to a massage, buying a new anything just because you want to, not because the one you have is falling apart? Do you consistently say no to yourself? Why?

If you felt you could benefit from therapy and could afford it but insurance wouldn't pay for it, would you do it anyway? I use this example intentionally, because the area of mental health is commonly regarded as optional rather than mandatory, and its results are primarily intangible. You may *feel* a whole lot better for having gone through therapy, but the outcome is not one you can measure in any real way beyond your sense of well-being. You'd probably have a different answer if I asked you what you'd do with a cancer diagnosis and no insurance. You'd find a way to pay for that shit, no matter what it took. The tangible outcome of that is much clearer. No treatment means certain death, while treatment means a chance at life.

The list of ways in which we can deny ourselves is nearly endless. You don't have to count the ways, but you should become familiar with the themes and thought processes that come up repeatedly in situations where you could decide to spend or not. If you treat money as the tool it is and use it to have experiences beyond paying for the basics, you allow it to play a powerful role in facilitating your enjoyment of life, which you deserve to do. Living in a constant state of scarcity, one in which you fear spending because you might need the money for something else, should lead you to ask yourself, "When will it ever be enough?" When will you be able to enjoy what you've worked for? Have you been selling yourself a story about how you'll enjoy it when you retire? You may not live that long, and what a kick in the balls that would be, to have hoarded your stash only to miss out on enjoying your life along the way instead of waiting for someday. It's also highly likely you're selling yourself a lie when you say you'll enjoy it when you retire. Your ingrained anxiety and programming regarding money isn't going to magically disappear at that point. In fact, it may become much more uncomfortable because, by definition, you are no longer earning but spending what you earned previously. You really believe you aren't going to be freaking out about burning through it too quickly, dialing back the dream vacation and maybe skipping out on the things you've been saying you wanted to do?

Before we get into your next steps, let's spend a little time thinking about how NOT to think about money. We are obsessed with the measurable in our society. How many or how much of anything you can buy or own is a demonstration of wealth, means, status, prestige, etc. When you earn a lot of money, it can bolster your confidence in yourself, but it can also create the gilded cage we've been talking about all along. It is critical that you know: **your earnings do not reflect your value.** Drill this into your head.

How many stories are out there about the now-famous person who started out with nothing but a shoestring and some tape in their basement, who developed the technology none of us want to live without now? Or the starving artist who lived under a bridge for a while and created something widely treasured for many to enjoy? The people with these stories didn't decide they were worthless because of their temporary circumstances. High achievers often get to the point where they tie their value up in their earning potential, so the thought of stepping away from that, even if just for a little while, is too overwhelming to contemplate. If you aren't making the money, what are you worth? Substitute role/title/position for earnings and take yourself through the same process. You aren't worth less because you aren't the director, VP, or CEO.

You have intrinsic value. **You are valuable just because you are.** You never look at your kid or someone else's and think, "God, look at you. Worthless. Can't even afford to buy a month's worth of groceries." It's just as ridiculous for you to have that thought process with respect to your own value.

To Don't:

- **Don't let limiting beliefs act as powerful brakes that keep you from moving** toward what you truly desire.
- **Don't tolerate the lack of prioritization that leads to useless busy-ness.** When you are too busy, it means no one thing is more important than another, and instead you are running around, trying to get it all done, and therefore allowing precious time you could be spending on *you* to go to waste.
- **Don't continue to accept in any way that your value is tied up in what you earn or own.** Your earnings do not reflect your value! Drill it into your head.

Do Instead:

- **Get familiar with your consistent thought patterns around time, money, and your value.** This will provide clarity on how you are participating in keeping yourself small.
- **PRIORITIZE.** You do have time. Make sure that what you spend your time on is aligned with where you want to go, and resist the urge to slip into reactivity. **You must be number one on your list of priorities.**
- **Learn to appreciate time and money as your friends.** Get out of the mental space of seeing them as elusive, and consciously create, through prioritization, an experience in which you see money as the tool for experiencing life that it is, and time as a resource that is at your fingertips if you treat it with respect rather than squandering it.

Summing Up

Appreciation of your self-worth is like laying the foundation for a home. It must be solid to support all the big beautiful stuff you want to build on top of it. It's time to uncover the ways in which you are undervaluing yourself. As always, try to maintain curiosity and suspend judgment. It takes conscious effort to sort through the experiences and expectations that brought you to where you are today. No matter how you were brought up, with a lot or not much, that experience comes with its own programming and impact on who you are today. A sense of shame may be lurking in the things you love that aren't valued by others. Identify negative beliefs, shame, and self-doubt so you can defuse them and move forward with acceptance that what you value is valid, no matter what anyone else thinks. Remember that your value has nothing to do with how much money you make. You have intrinsic value. Embrace it.

Time for the exercises that are going to get you on the path to clarity. Ask yourself the following:

1. Am I in the habit of prioritizing? Where am I on that list? Write down everything you do that contributes to feelings of being "busy" and assign themes to them, such as work, kids, sports, etc. Do NOT give up and decide that everything on the list has equal priority. Guilt about not putting any one of these in a top position may bubble up. Let it, and observe. You must be at the top of your list. This will make you feel guilty. You'll get over it when you experience the benefits of keeping yourself in that position, and it will positively reinforce your decision to do so.
2. What triggers feelings of guilt or shame for me? How are these feelings tied to events or old programming that need to be revisited? If this is a challenging area to think about, start by considering the following in terms of triggers:

    a. Does the thought of spending on myself, or taking time for myself, make me feel guilty? Am I letting down my workplace? My family?

b. If I don't want to run around to all these after-school activities, does that make me a bad parent?

c. What if I don't want to hang out with my extended family every Sunday?

d. I love (fill in the blank), but I can't spend money/time on that. It's not a good use of money/time.

3. What are my predominant thoughts about money? Have I been tying my value to what I make? How would it feel to not make as much money if I was providing value in other ways?

CHAPTER 9

Your Feelings Are Your Compass

"Don't make an emotional decision."
"Leave emotions of out this."
"Don't get emotionally involved."
"It's not personal, it's business."

We are relentlessly bombarded with the kind of stereotypical, cliché messages that encourage us to minimize our feelings in favor of logic and detachment from the most essentially human part of ourselves. We dismiss emotions as evil obstacles, to be ignored and stuffed down, then wonder why life doesn't *feel* the way we want it to. The irony is that every single thing we pursue in life, we go after because of how we believe it will feel when we've received, achieved, or accomplished it. Yet all too often, we find once we have reached the goal that we are underwhelmed, not at all feeling as inspired, accomplished, energized, or generally amazing as we had hoped to feel in the aftermath. This sets the high achiever up for serious disappointment. If what you strive for continues to elude you, what is the point of achieving?

The fundamentally flawed approach of dismissing emotions in favor of logic can do a tremendous amount of damage to us over a lifetime. Not only are we bombarded with the messages of the collective consciousness like the clichés I listed above, we are also taught that being emotional is equivalent to weakness and, worse yet, showing emotion makes you difficult to take seriously; clearly you are not stable enough to handle what life and work are handing to you. Better to hold it in, cry in private, rage when you've reached your limit, show love only to those who won't use it against you, and pretend that you are more like a robot than a human, stable and dependable under all conditions, generally emotionless and therefore safe to be around.

The external insistence that we dismiss our emotions is easily internalized, making it difficult to express emotions even when we are alone with our thoughts and feelings. How often do you allow yourself a good, hard, maybe even wailing, cry when you really need one? Do you quickly try to get yourself together? Get mad at yourself when you can't stop quickly enough? What do you say to yourself in those moments? If you don't allow yourself this outlet, are you telling yourself to keep it together? Why is it so damn important for us to keep ourselves under emotional control to the point where we feel it's wrong to let the barrier down, even if only occasionally?

The rejection of emotion plays a critical and undeniable role in how we come to stagnate at various points in our lives. It's how we end up in autopilot mode, resigned to the way it is, not truly processing or registering where we are or why. We can keep going indefinitely, disconnected from our core, because we've been taught since the beginning of time that "There's no crying in baseball, dammit!" We "suck it up," "keep putting one foot in front of the other," and "stay the course." Every message we get is that the goal is survival, and in order to do so, we continue to do what must be done, whether we like it or not. Our feelings don't factor into it. We just keep going, getting to the line in the sand we've drawn that means a milestone has been reached, perhaps celebrating it for a moment (if at all), then drawing the next line in the sand that we hope will bring more fulfillment than the last one did.

The truly mind-blowing aspect of our continual rejection of our emotions is that we deny the extent to which our emotions truly do serve us. How many times have you had a gut feeling about something or someone and decided to dismiss it in favor of logic and practicality? Maybe you even thought it would be considered socially incorrect to honor your gut feeling, because the other person's feelings took priority, or there were downstream implications with other connections to be concerned with. Recall the examples in which decision-making based on logic led to an undesired outcome and you said to yourself, "I knew it! I knew something was wrong. It didn't feel right, but I couldn't explain it, so I decided it was silly." It's highly likely you have many examples of how your inexplicable feelings about a person or situation were right on, but you were only able to see the proof you needed in hindsight.

We are especially dismissive of emotions we consider "bad." We try to talk ourselves out of the legitimacy of bad feelings, deciding our mood must be the issue, maybe the other person doesn't make good first impressions, your intuition can't be right because someone you like and respect thinks this person is awesome, how can this job offer be bad when it has all the things you said you wanted, etc. Emotions are not based on logic, but we often try to talk ourselves out of our emotions by using logic. The two cannot be compared, nor should they carry equal weight. Your feelings are by far the most important guiding light you have. They act as your compass and help steer you toward and away from situations, people, and circumstances if you will allow them to. It's when you don't allow your feelings to trump logic that you end up looking back in hindsight, wishing you had honored your feelings when you had the chance.

Get Intentional

With that foundation in mind, let's talk about ways you can start to undo your programming around the dismissal of your feelings that will impact your life holistically. In the chapter regarding achievement and your definition of success, we covered the ways in which your definition of success is heavily influenced by the world around you. Allowing your concept of success to be externally defined is one major way you participate in dismissing how you feel about anything. It's not about you, it's about how it looks, how it's measured, what it gets you, and so on. But because you've reached and, in many cases, surpassed the narrowly defined version of success and haven't found it to be all that, you know there's something missing from the equation. What's missing is your focus on how you want to feel, your new definition of success, and being intentional in making sure the goals you set align with where you want to be.

When I was in my own personal rat race, fully aware of the ways in which reaching goals was falling short of my personal expectations, I decided to ditch setting goals in favor of setting intentions. It seemed straightforward enough. As usual, I had done all the research about the various approaches for setting intentions, and I thought I was ready for it. I was pretty pumped up at the thought that I had found the magical key to unlocking the answer to my continual dissatisfaction. I sat down with my journal and did some brainstorming. I required a simple framework to keep myself from slipping back into goal-setting mode. The framework I came up with was this:

- **Goals** are measurable and somewhat short-term, able to be realized in months to a few years.
- **Intentions** are intangible and thematic, e.g. they create a backdrop of well-being in which to achieve the shorter-term goals.

It was enough to get me started. I came up with some good words to describe how I wanted to feel in general. When I got stuck with an idea that felt more like a goal, I would break it down.

Example: Greater responsibility.

Why? So I can expand my experience through leading others.

Why? So I can be recognized as a leader.

Why? So I can lead a team and be more directly invested in the greater outcome.

Why? To feel effective and like I'm making a larger contribution.

Conclusion: This is a goal, not an intention. Dang!

You may look at the answer to my last "why" and wonder why that didn't make the cut for the intention list. My need to feel effective was driven by a need for validation from others. The piece about making a larger contribution did actually make the cut, but it was too vague and didn't necessarily need to be tied to my job. I recognized it as a missing piece in my overall "success" that I wanted to find a way to create. I got back to work.

What's missing: Contribution to the greater good outside of myself.

What kind of contribution? Don't know yet.

This is where it gets really interesting. I could have let the fact that I didn't know what kind of contribution I wanted to make stop me in my tracks. But how you're going to get there is the last thing you need to be concerned with when you're creating your intentions. Onward.

What feeling/word encompasses contribution in whatever form it takes while fulfilling my need to do for others? Generosity.

Winner! Creating a life in which I could be generous was hugely important to me. Generosity is also multidimensional, so I could be generous with my time, connections, content, in whatever way it would feel good to give of myself in a valuable way. This one is still on my list, by the way.

If this sounds tricky, it's because it is! It requires you to think about what you're aiming for in a completely different way that's not tied to tangibility or a roadmap for how to achieve the outcome. You may be wondering, then, what's the point? The point is that how you're doing it now isn't working. Why not try something new and see how much further you get when you are free from the rigidity and parameters that limit you to a narrow path? The whole reason you get stuck to begin with is that you're trying to do it the way you've been told works, even though your own experience has taught you that that particular way will only get you so far. You stagnate when it's time to expand and grow, but your current approach keeps you from being able to do just that. It's time for another way, one in which you allow your feelings and who you are as a human being, rather than a career professional, drive you forward to the good things you hold yourself back from when you insist there is a right way and a kooky way.

I want you to know that this was SO HARD for me. I struggled mightily to do this. I would get to a point in the process, get all in my own head about it being too much of a departure from the way I knew to get things done, and I'd back off. Not for long, though, because I knew there was something to it, and it felt really good to have intentions that were bigger and broader than any goals I'd ever set before. In hindsight, I understand it's because I was attempting to do this work as one of the very first steps in the process, without the benefit of the background knowledge of the larger process I've shared to this point. I had to bounce around to determine where the holes were and then return to various steps to complete them when I felt equipped to do so. This won't be a cakewalk, but with the foundation you have now, you will be able to move toward intentionality rather than using goal-setting as the tool for moving forward.

Setting goals is not a bad thing, it's just not the most important thing. In fact, knowing which goals to set becomes much easier once you have a set of intentions. When contemplating a goal, you can think it through with your larger intentions in mind to decide whether it's a worthy goal and then guide you in how to set it, based on what you've determined you want for your life. Let's walk through another example to illustrate.

Stress has been a major issue for you at work. One of the intentions you've set is to move toward peace of mind. For you, peace of mind means being able to come home, be present for your family, take time to relax, and not feel tied to checking emails and texts, working late at night, etc. At the same time, it's been a goal of yours to get promoted. WHY do you want to be promoted? What comes with it, and does that list align with your intention to create peace of mind? Will you feel accomplished or serene when you've reached that goal? Why is the accomplishment important to you? Does it outweigh all the beautiful reasons why peace of mind is important to you?

Ultimately, if your goal doesn't align with your intentions, it doesn't make the cut. If you have to tie yourself in knots to justify your goal with a lot of "yeah, but" statements, you are likely slipping back into old programming and placing more weight on achievement than on what truly works for you. Does this mean you shouldn't have aspirations for your professional life? No. But it does mean your aspirations for your professional life MUST hold space for you to have the experience you want, and if where you are isn't a conducive environment, then it's time to explore options beyond where you are today.

Once you have a set of intentions and goals that are in line with those intentions, you are ready to take it to the next level, to go big and dream about how life will feel to you with this new approach. As was discussed in the chapter on fear, this can be an incredibly scary step, to envision the life defined according to your desires, because what if you can't have it? What if it eludes you? Remember, when fear shows up in this way, its intent is protective—if you don't try, it says, you won't fail. Be okay with settling, it says, so you won't have to experience the disappointment and loss of the dream that you were okay without, because it's more painful to see it, feel it, taste it, and then not get it. But being "okay" and "fine" are no longer enough. Idealize your life, know that you can have whatever you put your mind to, and don't limit yourself by staying imprisoned in your current framework, with your outdated programming and fear-based decision-making. You are at the point in this journey where you have a choice to make. Resign yourself to being fine and living a safe life where the most you can hope for is oscillation between boredom and contentment, or say fuck it, raise the bar way up high, and give yourself something to strive for, where the result is a life in which you are more often than not in a place of energy, inspiration, and joy.

It's your right to experience the positive heights of emotion; it's a choice not to pursue those heights. It's a valid choice, as long as you are willing to accept that you must be clear on what you're willing to give up. If being okay is good enough for you, then it means you are compromising and you no longer have the option of complaining about your circumstances. All the power lies within you to make the choice. Make the choice knowingly and accept the responsibility that comes with the choice you've made. If you come to a point where you are no longer willing to compromise and settle, pick yourself up and commit to raising your expectations and doing what comes with that commitment to make it to where you want to be.

After I did my little dance with setting intentions and determining which goals were valid for moving me forward, I reached a natural plateau. I had some things down; I had a much more empowered set of expectations for my life, but still had no real and complete framework around those expectations. I could look at each intention and know what it entailed, but a bigger picture of life including all of that in aggregate hadn't yet formed in my mind. It was kind of like learning to waltz, in that awkward three-beat way that goes against our natural expectation of rhythm in four beats, knowing the sequence of steps but not enough to do actually do an entire waltz to music just yet. I had the new way of thinking and the steps, but I hadn't figured out how to bring it together in a larger vision. It was time to daydream and experiment with a very different picture of life than the one I had been living and had resigned myself to.

With each new step in the process, I discovered that I had to overcome the same barriers, finding that it was my default to pick apart what I was seeing, registering the limitations, worrying about how I was going to make it happen, and fearing that I was being unrealistic. However, by this time, my ability to quickly navigate and overcome the programming was improving, strengthened by the practice of doing all the other exercises that came before it. You will find that, the more you push yourself in the direction of the new way, the more second nature it becomes, until you do it so quickly and naturally that you barely register the effort. It's like forming any habit or ritual; you do it until it you don't have to think about it much, but with a level of awareness that keeps you from slipping into zombie mode as you do it. I had some stuttering starts as I eased myself through my own objections to the vision that was forming. I did the evaluation of my intentions against my current reality, trying to determine if I could move toward that vision while remaining in my career, or if a change was required. I would start to go down the rabbit hole of what kinds of jobs I could do, then would have to back up out of it and remember that the *how* wasn't important just yet. I could see where the benefits and drawbacks of staying put came into play, and by this time, I was so much more in tune with myself that I started to sense that I had a calling of some kind. I wasn't sure what it was, but I knew that, the more I continued to be unfocused on the *how*, the closer I would get to the calling, allowing it to come into focus instead of ramming myself down a path because I couldn't handle the uncertainty.

Purpose vs. Profession

I am not suggesting that you have to know what your Purpose is or have a Calling. It's also not necessary for the way you earn money to be tied to what fulfills you. But if you want to go from ho-hum to fantastic, it is a requirement that you make space in your life for what lights you up. Love to cook? Inspired by hanging out with kids in need of role models? Are you a closet artist? Someone who's all fired up by standing up for those who can't stand up for themselves? How are you (if you are at all) giving yourself an outlet to express the fundamental pieces of who you are? If you're not, why not? Do you have the mistaken belief that, because something is not a money-making activity, it shouldn't be prioritized? You've been prioritizing money-making for a while now...how's that working out for you? Give yourself permission to spend time doing what you love. Make it a priority and see how that creates space in your brain and heart for the flow of inspiration, creativity, and dreaming. Who knows what being in a totally different state of mind for the time you set aside will unlock for you? Whether you believe it or not, you are a creative person. Creativity isn't limited to artistic talent; it's the ability to innovate in any given area, whether it's the arts, business, technology, marketing, etc. Take the narrow-ass guardrails off your brain and let it go off-roading for a bit. See what you can tap into, and give yourself the opportunity to broaden your horizons through the activities that energize you. At the very least, you'll be adding value to your life, even if all that comes of it is that you get to spend time doing what you love. You'll have more energy for everything else in your life when you give this gift to yourself.

We've talked about the good that intentionality and positive feelings can bring you, but it's important to recognize that what we often refer to as negative emotions play an equally important role. When you are down, depressed, despairing, angry, uncomfortable, bored, or restless, those feelings act as your internal alarm system. They tell you something is not right. Unfortunately, the first tendency can be to avoid or talk ourselves out of the bad feelings, because we either don't want to or don't know how to identify the root cause so that the problem can be addressed. The issues at play can be multidimensional, making it exhausting to try and figure out how to get to the bottom of what's happening. Acknowledge the "negative" feelings and treat them as your warning signals, your friends trying to wake you up to the fact that something in your life isn't working. The more out of alignment you are with your core being, the worse you will feel. When you begin to take corrective action, as we've been discussing throughout the book, you reclaim the power to make your life the way you want it, and you'll spend less time in the warning emotions. You're human, so you'll never be free of discomfort, but discomfort is the key to growth. You don't know it's time to change until it gets uncomfortable. Feelings are your friends. All of them—the good, the bad, and the ugly. Learn to work with them, to address what they are telling you, instead of against them, and your life will change for the better.

To Don't:

- **Don't permit logic to trump emotion.** The two are entirely separate; the use of one to negate the other is ineffective and leads to weakened decision-making.
- **Don't continue to emphasize tangibility**. You already know that all the measurable things you've accomplished haven't fulfilled you.
- **Don't get caught up in asking how** you will manifest the life you envision. Once you figure out the *what,* the *how* will follow, if you'll allow yourself to let go of the need for control.

Do Instead:

- **Focus on your feelings.** They are your internal guidance system. Resist the urge to analyze your way out of what your feelings guide you toward.
- **Set intentions before you set goals**. Intentions are the foundation for your goals that provide clarity and a check/ balance to make sure the actions you prioritize are in line with your desired life.
- **Give weight to the intangibles in your life**—how you want to feel, what you want to experience, who you spend your time with, how you spend that time, etc. What cannot be measured is the key to the fulfillment that has been missing from your life.

Summing Up

Your feelings are the internal guidance system that will lead you if you'll let it. Up to this point in your life, you've spent way too much time worrying about logic, practicality, expectations, and making sure that you are perceived as a person of value and worth, without taking the time to make sure you are internally secure in that knowledge. When you dismiss your feelings or rationalize your way to a contrary position or decision, you often live and learn. In hindsight, you see that your feelings were correct about how to proceed in a given situation, even though you couldn't explain why you knew that to be the case. Using logic to contradict emotion doesn't work. The two are not equivalent, and the more time you spend honoring your feelings and trusting your instincts, the more aligned your decisions will be. You will rarely be disappointed in decision-making that comes from your gut/heart. No more stomping on your emotions or letting logic rule the day, unchallenged by your emotions. Examine your feelings, look at how you're trying to talk yourself out of them, and fast-forward mentally to the possible outcomes to see what realizations you can project having if you make the logic-based, rather than emotion-based, decision. Does that mean the outcome will always be perfect? Not necessarily. We sometimes have lessons to learn and learn them we will, even if we do our best to make the aligned decision. It's not about perfection, but about making the best decision with the information you have at the time. The information you have in the form of your own intuition is powerful and should be given the weight it deserves.

Here are some ways to get started with putting feelings in the driver's seat.

1. How do you set goals today? Do you have a tendency to be one-dimensional, e.g. focused on work and neglecting the rest of life?
2. Do your goals have predominantly measurable outcomes? How do you feel when you meet measurable goals? Is it everything you hope it to be, or is something missing? How do you expect to feel when you meet those goals?

3. Set your intentions. How do you want life to feel? Come up with three to five words that reflect your general desires for life and make them the framework for how to proceed with goal-setting. Goals must contribute to your intentions. If they don't, tweak the goal so that accomplishing it feeds your intentions, or ditch it and come up with a different one.
4. Review the examples in the chapter that walk through how to know if your intentions are broad enough and whether they are sufficiently internal. In other words, do not pick words/intentions that create dependency on outside factors in order for you to have met your intentions. If you say you want to feel accomplished, that's highly tangible and leaves you open to whether others believe you've met that mark. If your life has been chaotic, maybe serenity or peace are on the intentions list. See the difference? Question yourself until you get to the answer that reflects what you want from your heart and soul and that you have the power to create.
5. Let your feelings guide you. Do not dismiss them, do not overanalyze them. Sit with them, ask yourself how you'll feel if you go against your instincts to make a different decision. Will you have peace of mind? Will you be sure that you did the right thing, or are you setting yourself up for nagging doubt and waiting for things to fall apart? What are the consequences of making the decision logically or emotionally? Come up with them to the best of your ability, then make your decision, as informed as you can be about the outcomes you are allowing, based on the way you are deciding. THIS IS NOT ABOUT GIVING YOURSELF PERMISSION TO MAKE SHITTY DECISIONS BASED ON FEELINGS THAT ARE INAPPROPRIATE OR HAVE SERIOUS LONG-TERM CONSEQUENCES THAT YOU CAN'T TAKE BACK. Owning how you feel means you do not abdicate responsibility and escape reality because feelings. "I'm doing it because it feels good" is sometimes good enough, but not when you're being shortsighted, hurting someone else, putting someone else at risk, or generally being reckless in order to avoid what's going on in your life.

6. Once you have your intentions (framework) and goals (short-term roadmap), start dreaming about your vision. What do you want your life to look and feel like, generally speaking? Where do you go? How do you spend your free time? What are your relationships like? How do you feel when you're engaged in work? Do not get so narrow that you go into the details; stay at the experiential level and visualize.

CHAPTER 10

What About Your Friends?

At the height of my professional misery, one thing that kept me going was that I had company in my sorry state. So many people I respected and enjoyed working with were just as unhappy as I was. We would plan lunch or happy hour to escape the office and go someplace where we could vent our frustration, but not before looking over our shoulders and darting our eyes across the room to ensure that no one else from our company was seated nearby and could overhear what we said. We would linger after meetings in conference rooms, door shut, and let it all flow, right after we picked up the phone receiver and hung it up, just in case we had forgotten to do so. Having a bitching session recorded for posterity was not high on the list of things to do before you die. It's fascinating to consider the state of paranoid watchfulness that was accepted as a normal matter of course. Duh—of course we hang up the phone three times and scan the room twice before we start whispering to each other about what's wrong in the land of work. Doesn't everyone?

Such conversations were like a drink of water after wandering around thirsty on a warm day. The problem was that it was kind of like a dirty drink of water, one that didn't completely refresh, but was just enough to keep you going, accepting the shit outwardly, screaming about it inwardly, and showing at least a little emotion privately. It's a coping mechanism that we humans adopt to make it easier to tolerate our shitty situations, whether those situations are professional or personal. Venting without a plan for change is an incredibly unhealthy way of dealing with whatever it is that's keeping you stuck. Venting gives way to more venting. Expressing your rage and frustration may temporarily provide some relief, but, in reality, you're stoking the fire of those emotions, ensuring that they burn brightly once again when a sufficient number of triggers arrive to feed the blaze. Venting is not a plan. It's a pattern, and a damaging one at that.

When you vent with others who share your feelings, you create a tribe of the miserable who understand one another and bond through that understanding. It can bring you closer to your coworkers and friends, creating an empty comfort and community that's built upon your misery. I'll say that again—it builds a sense of community around shared misery. Is that what you really want? To bond over what sucks? To make it to the next happy-hour or conference-room conversation that will keep you going, treading water in the same place indefinitely, able to tolerate it because you're not alone? The recognition of what's not right and bonding over it are not a problem if you plan to take action to improve your lot. But let's be honest here—you're doing a whole lot of tolerating and not a lot of acting to make it better when you participate in this cycle.

When I had my exit plan in place, I didn't share it with many people. People like to gossip and, even if they didn't do it intentionally, I didn't want to risk exposing my plans before I was ready to give notice. By that point, I had participated in more venting sessions than I could count, with people both inside and outside of my organization. We would lament the current course and trajectory, talk about what we would do differently, know that our words would fall on deaf ears (in many cases because they already had), and live to fight another day. I had done so much personal development work over the last couple of years that I could see the damage I was doing to myself by continuing to complain. I was done complaining. I had reached my conclusions. It was time to get the eff out. I didn't want to alienate those I cared about, so I would still make time to listen, but the way I participated began to morph. I was no longer on the "I know, right?!" train. I would listen, then ask questions meant to spur the other to action. I would ask things like: Are you going to say something? What would you do differently? Can you create the plan for how you'd do it and set up some time to share it? You've been talking about this for a long time—why are you still putting up with it? How long will you allow this to go on? You are talented and have options; why do you insist on staying in this position?

The effects of this line of questioning worked and didn't work. As you know by now, you have to be ready to take on the pieces of your life that aren't working for you. I can point to examples all day long that show evidence of what's out of whack, but if the receiver isn't ready to do the work, they won't do it. It raised their awareness about what they were tolerating, but more often than not, what immediately followed the acknowledgment of their situation was some variation of "I don't have a choice." Well. That's certainly not true, but you can't push people toward empowered action. They must take the steps to empower themselves. It was hardly possible to take that on in a five-minute office drive-by, as much as I wanted to. There were some people I believed in so fervently (and still do), and wanted something better for them so badly, I would find myself continually following them into their own rabbit hole to see what I could do to drag them out. It was wasted energy. I couldn't want it for them more than they wanted it for themselves. But *you* can and should want it badly enough for yourself that you stop participating in the tribal comfort of staying stuck.

Venting vs. Doing

Who you hang out with and what you talk about matters, personally and professionally. If you are hanging out with the bitches-a-lot-but-doesn't-do-shit-about-it crowd, you are making a choice to stay in your rut. I'm not suggesting you suddenly back out of every happy hour or social situation with the crew that complains. Actually, I'm suggesting you keep going, at least for a little while, and observe how you are a part of this cycle. Watch the people you're with. How do they seem to feel about their circumstances? How many times have they brought up the same situations and complaints? Are they pointing fingers, blaming. or playing the victim in the situation? Are they disempowered, acting as if there is no way out, no options available? Think about how you would normally chime in and do the same. What would you be talking about and how would you be talking about it? How can you do it differently this time, in a way that describes the problem, but also the choices and options available for addressing it? How can you make yourself accountable to take action on one or more of those options? Could you tell them, "The next time we meet, I'll have an update on how it went when I tried X or Y"? You don't have to do what everyone else is doing.

If it makes you uncomfortable to consider being the one who does it differently, why? If you're thinking, "That would be super annoying to the group, trying to be all problem-solve-y when all they really want to do is complain because it's how they bond," then stop right there. That's an important piece of information. If this group of people wants to complain, then it's not a group you should be spending a lot of time with, especially when you are so vulnerable, early in the process of addressing the outdated programming and patterns that have brought you to where you are. There's a good chance someone in that group is going to be inspired or awakened by your approach. He or she may not speak up in that moment but may reach out to you afterward to talk more. You need like-minded people on your journey. As was discussed in the chapter on fear, fear of being alone is powerful. Beginning to separate yourself from the way things have been done with the people you've done them with can feel risky, as if you are inviting isolation. Remember that what you are really doing is creating the space in your life for the like-minded to come into the picture.

Sticking with the known, when it comes to personal and professional groups, is a powerful way to stay in your place. It normalizes your experience when other people feel similarly to you. It goads you into accepting the status quo, because it's everyone's status quo—why are you so special that you believe you should have a different experience? You're all talented, successful people, right? It must just be the way it is if everyone is in the same boat. If you've already moved past that and do believe you deserve to have better, continuing to hang out with the resigned folks can pull you back to where you started quickly and easily.

When you meet resistance and skepticism, your tendency early in the transformative journey is to let the self-doubt rise back up, rekindling your own resistance and skepticism. It's far better to be alone with your thoughts than to share them with people who won't support you on your path.

To Share or Not to Share

As much as we've talked about open communication, it's vital that you choose carefully with whom to share your personal development journey. You are like a tender shoot that's just emerged from the soil. The conditions around you must be as ideal as possible to foster your growth. Letting others in can quickly upset the balance of those conditions. You likely already have a good idea of whom you could safely share your plans with, and if you aren't sure, that's okay. You can test the waters a bit and see what kind of reaction you get before you go all in.

When I got serious about making some changes in my life, I knew with certainty who would be supportive. For others, it would be trickier. The certain-of-support conversations went something like this:

Me: "I don't want to do this anymore. I've decided I'm going to find a way to leave my job and do something else. I'm not sure what, but I'm working on it."

Awesomely awesome friends: "You can do it. You can do anything. I believe in you. Now tell me how you're doing all of this. I'm intrigued."

For real, it was that easy. I knew these people would be supportive, but I did expect a bit more of a "Wait…what?" reaction, and it never came. It was humbling. Their belief in me at that moment when I still had my own doubts had a powerfully bolstering effect on my resolve. The people who know and love me believed in me. They saw something in me that I didn't even fully realize yet. Their support and steadiness had the effect of cement poured over a foundation. Perhaps most importantly, these friends weren't yet on their own self-discovery missions, yet my start on that path didn't make them defensive. It interested them. They wanted to know how I got started and, before long, they started down their own paths. If you're feeling discouraged, not sure if you have friends like this in your life at this time, don't despair. Your standards for friendship and connection are going to evolve and improve throughout this process, and you will have friends like this if you don't now. Believe it or not, people you don't know well at all can quickly become some of your biggest and most ardent supporters. We'll talk more about that a little later in the chapter.

I was much more hesitant to share my plans with family members, most coworkers, and some of my friends from back in the day. When it came to family, I knew that many of them, especially my parents and their siblings, wouldn't understand. To them, I'd achieved the American dream. What more could I possibly want? Why would I take such a risk? Because these were thoughts I'd already processed and in some ways was still dealing with, I didn't need the pile-on at that point. I also knew that I didn't want to get into justifying my position. There was simply no need for anyone else to understand. I got it, the people I'd chosen to trust with this information got it, and I didn't need the naysaying in my head. I kept it to myself for a long time, and, even when I did share, I did so sparingly, providing only the details I was comfortable with and not responding to questions that tried to make me demonstrate the rationale for the decision. Nope. My reasons were mine alone. I didn't need anyone else to get it, and neither do you. Your reasons are valid whether other people understand them or not. Share with those you trust to be your supporters, and keep it to yourself when it comes to those who won't.

It can be confusing to keep details from the people you love, who believe they have your best interests at heart. The hard part is that it can be your parents, siblings, and closest friends who challenge you because they don't want you to make a mistake and throw it all away while, from their perspective, you're clearly having some kind of mental break from reality. What's harder still is that this type of reaction may be defensive, born of a sense that they lack the drive and determination to do the same for their own lives, so your willingness to be on this journey is a threat to their sense of comfort. They'd prefer that you stay where you are, with them, so they can continue to feel okay about their lives, settling for the ho-hum. If you don't stay there with them, it's an uncomfortable challenge to their position, and they'd rather not go there, thank you. Best for all if you just stay put. Several of my longtime friends were in this category as well.

Friends: "What have you been up to? What's new?"
Me: "I've been doing all this self-analysis and I've decided I'm going to leave my job to become a coach."
Friends: Stare.
Me: Waiting for it…
Friends: "Well, that's interesting! Anyway, the other day…"

The reaction was disappointing, but not unexpected. Ultimately, it served me to have witnessed it. I knew the people who reacted this way weren't necessarily going to be an integral part of my life moving forward. My path had diverged to the point where they were no longer comfortable around me, and I was no longer okay with spending hours engaged in relatively small talk or repetitive conversations about the same troubles and woes that remained unaddressed. It took me a while to get to the point where I recognized it as a neutral outcome rather than a bad one. There's no right or wrong choice. You can choose to move forward or choose to stay put, but when you're not making the same choice, your paths, by necessity, will diverge and you will go down the other fork in the road. One is not more valid than the other, but one does foster more growth, and that was the path I had dedicated myself to.

My work relationships were a mixed bag. I had those I considered my true friends, and those who I knew would react more like family or some of my friends. Because I was dealing with high achievers, I understood that hearing my plans to do something different could trigger feelings of defensiveness, as if my plans were a rejection of the life my coworkers were resigned to. I trusted a few coworkers with my plans and received mixed responses.

Me: "I'm planning to get out of here, do my own thing."

Coworker type 1: "OMG, you're so lucky. I'm so jealous. What are you going to do? You're so brave. I wish I had the balls to try something like that."

Coworker type 2: "Really? Why? Where else are you going to make this much money? Why can't you just go on more vacations, take more breaks? The money is too good. And besides, won't you miss the people?"

The first type was supportive and longed for change in their own lives but were generally still in a place where they felt their only option was to stay. The second type was fully aware of the challenges that came with the corporate life and complained about it yet had accepted it as the trade-off for having money and security. I had already moved past that point. I wasn't willing to make that trade any longer, and I didn't continue to share details with those in this camp. Not because I didn't trust them, but because I knew mutual understanding was missing, which made the exchanges a waste of energy.

Separate from the Pack

This part of the journey, where you begin to separate yourself, can be one of the toughest stretches as you learn who you can trust, who will support you, who will try to keep you in place, and who will decide you are an alien life-form for daring to dream of a different life. You will be humbled, relieved, disappointed, triggered, angry, sad, and at times, isolated. KEEP GOING. What you learn about yourself and what you expect for your relationships during this time is priceless and is one of the golden keys to creating the life you've dreamed of. Can you imagine a life in which you are surrounded by people who believe in you and believe in themselves enough to do this with you? It's life-changing to go from conversations based in resignation and low expectations to dreaming excitedly about what comes next as you raise your expectations and dare to go after what lights you up.

By far, one of the most humbling experiences of this journey for me has been meeting new people who became instant fans and supporters of mine. People who, after one meeting, immediately wanted to talk about how we could work together, how I could support them or their teams, who they could introduce me to, how they could help me get to where I wanted to be. Seriously. This has happened to me after one exposure more times than I can count. These people are now part of my network, and we continue to talk about plans for the future and how we are going to help each other get there. Perhaps most surprisingly, it took hardly any time at all for these people to come into my life. Less than six months after leaving my corporate job, I met at least five people who have been playing this role for me ever since, and the impact has been exponential, as they continue to connect me with more like-minded people. Within a few months, my network expanded and today is almost unrecognizable, compared to where it was when I started this journey. Once you show up authentically, people can see you and show up to support you. But it doesn't happen magically. You need to do your part.

Not only should you look for the like-minded, but search for and find people who inspire you, who have qualities you admire and that you want to continue to hone in yourself. I'm very fortunate that many of the people closest to me, from the friends I knew would have my back to the new people who have come into my life, embody the supportive aspect and, in addition, they themselves are people I admire, with as much to offer me as they believe I have to offer them. Mutual respect and a shared vision for a better life can go a long way toward forging bonds between people very quickly. Be both deliberate in your efforts to connect with such people and open to seeing who comes into your life once you've decided on your new path.

To Don't:

- **Don't make a habit of venting with like-minded friends and coworkers.** It may bring temporary relief, but stop bonding over what sucks and work on a plan for improving your situation.
- **Don't continue to normalize your experience** by comparing it with the experience of others. Just because they are miserable, too, doesn't mean it's okay.
- **Don't trumpet your plans to anyone and everyone.** You are vulnerable at this stage in the process. The doubt of others can poison your determination.

Do Instead:

- **Find people who are more interested in creating their realities than complaining about them.** Look for those who are already in a place you aspire to be, and identify the people in your life who want to do this along with you.
- **Show up. Be authentic. Let people see you.** It will bring in those who are good companions for you on this journey and clear out those who aren't.
- **KEEP GOING.** If you are experiencing fear or a sense of isolation, know that it will pass.

Summing Up

Who you spend time with and what you talk about is hugely important to the quality of your life. If the time spent is more steeped in complaints and reliving the repeated patterns that have been holding you back, you are creating more of the same. It takes concerted effort to break habitual cycling in the areas of your life where you truly desire improvement but are steeped in the status quo instead of finding ways to move forward. It can be scary to consider moving forward without those you've come to depend on personally and professionally. Fear of being alone is powerful and can stop you in your tracks if you let it. Understand that any isolation you experience is temporary. As you move away from what no longer works for you and start showing up differently, the people who more closely match where you want to be will start to appear, as if by some mystical force. No matter what your beliefs are, know that when you show up for yourself, others will show up for you, as well. It's pretty much just a law of the universe, so whether you believe in it or not makes no difference. You'll see.

Start by taking small steps toward evaluating the nature of your most common interactions and looking for your new crew, personally and professionally.

1. Observe your current interactions. What are the topics of conversation? Is there a lot of complaining but little action? Is there a theme of resignation, like there's no choice but to endure?
2. Who can you reach out to? Can you find local people on LinkedIn, join a networking group, find a cause you care about and attend a meeting? Make it a point to meet new people; make space in your calendar to meet for coffee or a happy hour drink. Identify two groups of people to reach out to within the next thirty days and get it scheduled.
3. Get out your journal and write down some thoughts on the kinds of people you would be energized by spending time with. Are they inspired by their work or a cause? Are they positive and empowered? Are they fun to be around? Chances are you have at least one or two people like this in

your life, whether at work or at home. Make it a point to connect individually and share where you are. You could be pleasantly surprised by a deeper connection with someone who's been in your orbit and will support you on your path.

4. Stop participating in complaining sessions. If you'd like the perspective of others on a particular challenge you're facing, present it that way. Set the tone for finding a solution, rather than just bitching to get it off your chest, and help others do the same. Listen and ask questions that could help them. If this is the hundredth time you've heard the same story, ask what they are doing to make it better. The way they respond to the question will tell you whether they are going to stay attached to their struggle or if they are willing to take action to get to a better place. For responses that reflect the former, limit the time you give to those people going forward. Time is precious, and you have a lot of growing to do. Give your time to those who are invested in their own growth as well.

5. Be open. You never know how a single meeting will impact you moving forward. For several months, I made a promise to myself that I would meet with every single person who asked me to do so. I did and don't regret it for an instant. There isn't a single person I would have chosen not to spend that time with. I learned a lot about myself through meeting new people. It will broaden your horizons and get you thinking about a bigger picture to spend time with people who are not inside your current experience.

CHAPTER 11

Stay in Your Lane

Have you ever had the experience of watching someone make a series of decisions so bad that it was like watching a slow-motion train wreck? A situation where someone did something at work that was so inappropriate that it blew your mind, so you promptly got together with other mind-blown coworkers behind closed doors so you could ask each other "Did you see that?? WTF was he thinking?" If it's a juicy enough tidbit, you'll stay on it for a while, analyzing, discussing, wondering, and perhaps even feeling secretly entertained by what took place. You may jump on other forms of communication, texting and instant messaging, the drama a temporary respite from the usual routine as the word about the latest happenings begins to spread through the organization.

We all have innumerable examples of such happenings in our personal and professional lives. The curious (and petty) side of us really wants to know what happened, recounted with the glorious details that give us something to dwell upon, practically salivating at the scandal of it all. Part of it is human nature; gossip is an ancient form of communication that people have indulged in probably since there were three people upon the earth, two of the three no doubt whispering behind cupped hands about the third when the poor bugger was out of earshot. Sometimes the retelling of such stories is harmless, particularly when what occurred was funny and the people involved participate in the retelling themselves. But most of the time, these stories are shared in a way that harms both the subject of the anecdote and the people involved in talking about it afterwards.

You might be wondering "What's the harm?" in indulging in such behaviors. There are many, actually. And before we go on, I want to make it clear that I am not a purist. We are all human, and sometimes the behavior of others is truly fascinating. If you can stay in a place of curiosity when you consider what someone else has done, it's okay to contemplate, with empathy, what may have driven them to do what they did. We can and do learn from others throughout our lives. If you treat it as an opportunity for enlightenment, by all means, proceed. The challenge is that there is a very fine line between curiosity and nosiness. Nosy is when you want all the juicy details because you're entertained by the thought of someone else's plight; for obvious reasons, this is no good. Treating others as you wish to be treated should always be front and center of how you operate. You wouldn't want to be on the receiving end, having people be in your business, if the situation was reversed, so keep that in mind when you decide how to participate in dissecting the actions of others.

Withhold Judgment

One of the most damaging elements of this behavior is that it puts you in the position of judging others. I say this with the full confession that I am a recovering Judger-in-Chief. For real. I used to judge people up one side and down the other, and to what end? I grew up in an environment in which judging others was practically a sport, and I know many of you have had the same experience, whether it started with your family or with a circle of friends. The corrosive and universally destructive belief that it's our place to do this where others are concerned is difficult to escape; bonds are often forged in these moments of judging and looking down on others. Consider the cliques you saw or were a part of growing up. Wasn't it practically a requirement to think of yourselves as cooler than thou? Judgment and entitlement are built into those structures, forming the nasty habit early in life, easily continuing into adulthood if left unchecked. There are thousands of reasons why it's not okay to be in the habit of judging, but let's look at the most important reasons as they relate to your personal development journey:

- It's a distraction which allows you to focus on others rather than yourself.
- It's misinformed because you aren't the other person and can't truly put yourself in their shoes to understand why they chose to do something.
- It enables the false sense that you are better than the other, dimming your ability to feel compassion and empathy for others.
- It's a habit that consumes your mental space, leaving little room for you to focus on you, what you want to create, etc.
- It's a fundamentally negative energy that has the unfortunate effect of keeping you in an energetically negative place, rather than keeping that space open for what's good, inspiring, energizing, creative, etc.
- It's just none of your damn business.

I had a lot of anger issues as an adolescent. The expression of anger and rage in my household was a regular occurrence, and a natural extension of that was judgment. The anger was directed in a way that judged the other, often harshly, and unfortunately for my family, this was an ancestral pattern, one passed down from the generations before. I heard words aimed at loved ones with calculation, intended to be as hurtful as possible and to incite a reaction so that the battle someone craved would arise, providing an outlet for deep despair and pain. I refer to the ancestral pattern because the pain wasn't about just the lives of those involved, but the lives of a culture and society that had been oppressed and, at the time of my childhood, was engaged in a devastating war. My parents left their home country in large part because of oppression and unease about what might happen next. They left behind their families and way of life, and, just a few years after that, the country was embroiled in political unrest, the overthrow of a secular government and its replacement by a theocracy, and a war fueled by the West that decimated the population of men and destroyed families. They didn't just leave their homeland. Their homeland essentially disappeared, leaving in its place a culture and way of life that was completely foreign to them. Essentially, they were left without roots, new to one country while the old had been dismantled. As an adult, I have empathy for my parents and their families, that they had to endure such terrifying and tragic circumstances, helpless to do anything to stop it. I understand the anger and rage that had nowhere to go but out, directed toward whomever was close enough to take it. But the damage it did was very real, and as a young adult I realized I had a choice. I could continue on the path of anger and despair, or I could find a way to move forward in a less painful way. I started seeing a psychologist my senior year in high school, and that experience laid the foundation for changing my reaction to the world.

As I shared earlier, I learned from my first therapy experience that anger is a secondary emotion, there to mask something deeper and scarier that I didn't feel equipped to deal with. Once I realized that my anger was masking hurt, I could see that I was injured and scared, afraid to be me. Being me meant being abused, dismissed, overlooked, and ignored. Of course, those weren't the only things I had ever felt or experienced in my life. But everything I had accomplished and "proved" was to contradict those feelings that were buried deep inside me and that anger provided a quick defense against. Anger meant I didn't have to look at or process any of that, and it also protected me from inviting more of the same by repelling anyone who tried to interact with me. Anger was my defense mechanism. I knew I had a lot to work on, but it was like someone had given me the key to the box with the answers, the box I had been kicking around in my rage, ignorant of the fact that it held the answers.

My own pain laid the foundation for directing anger and judgment at others. The people who knew me and loved me didn't see this reality about me. One of the things about me, for better or worse, is that I came across as self-confident and competent even at a young age. Even today, people are frequently shocked by my backstory, having assumed that I am who I am because I'm one of those people for whom life is easy. Chances are, you've heard the same comments about you or have thought them about someone else. The point is that you aren't in someone else's experience. You have no idea what has happened or is going on in their life. When you judge and make a habit of picking apart the actions of others, it's highly likely you're hiding from your own underlying (and perhaps hidden) issues and what you should be focused on. Focusing on other people's shit is a way of avoiding your own. A major realization for me was that I had to accept that other people aren't built like me. I can't expect them to do things the way I would or to confront the things I have. Their way isn't wrong or worse. It just is. You can't make people be ready to tackle what's not right in their lives. Their decision to stay put is their decision, whether you agree with it or not, as we just said about who you surround yourself with.

Managing Triggers

When you look at what others are doing and are triggered by it, take a breath and remind yourself that, although you have thoughts on how they could improve their lives, a) you can't force it on them, b) you can't want it more than they do, and c) it distracts you from what *you* personally should be working on. We can all fall into this trap when it comes to our closest friends and family members, getting all bent out of shape about a situation or circumstance that's not good enough for them, that they could be doing more to help themselves with, etc. Stop judging. You don't have to agree with it. They aren't obligated to take your advice. They don't have to be ready to deal with whatever it is, even if it's holding them apart from their potential. Back off. Be supportive. Listen. Acknowledge where they are, while being willing to point out that they can choose to be in a different place, without jumping all over them. You can decide not to allow them to re-cover old ground repeatedly, instead reminding them that they have a choice, and asking them what they could do differently to create a better outcome. You get to decide what works for you, and they get to decide what works for them.

At times, there are truly triggering things occurring in the world that you cannot simply ignore. It's not okay to pretend you don't see it or to dismiss options for participating in improving the situation because you believe you don't have the power. This is the single most bullshit idea any of us possesses. Just think about how many times the actions of a single person have impacted your life. The kind word, the understanding, the quick favor, the willingness to help, even with something seemingly small? Because big, highly impactful actions done on a grand scale are what we hear about collectively, we make the false assumption that smaller deeds are insignificant. Consider the collective power of donating to a cause. You can donate food, clothing, money, and time, and, if many others do the same, the impact is exponential. Add your effort, in whatever form works for you, to the efforts of others. Together you make a difference. Individually, do what you are able to do in the moment to make life a little better for someone when the opportunity arises. If you're not sure what to do, consider what you would want in that scenario and do it. There's no one right action, but don't make a habit of taking no action. A world full of people who have no interest in the well-being of others is not a world any of us wants to live in. Be a part of making it better in whatever way you can.

Generally speaking, the best and most productive policy is to stay in your lane. Do not approach this policy narrowly, with the assumption that you are to worry about you only. On the contrary, this is about doing what is most beneficial for all in a way that harnesses how you personally can contribute to that benefit. Let's cover a few examples of how staying in your lane could look in various situations.

- There's a story circulating at work about a coworker you know, whose behavior in a recent meeting was a bit over the top. He got angry about a situation with a client and let his anger out in the form of some choice words and behavior that were not typical for him. People are speculating about why he lost it, because this is some juicy shit. How can you stay in your lane?
    - Don't participate. Make a simple statement like, "It's hard to know what may be going on with him, but I hope he's okay." Then leave, or otherwise remove yourself. If the person in question is someone you

know well enough to reach out to, do so in a way that feels appropriate under the circumstances. Perhaps a quick message like, "I heard about what happened. I hope you're doing okay. Let me know if you want to talk about it." Leave it at that.

- You're having a drink with a friend who is complaining about her husband AGAIN. You have spent many such conversations talking about what she can do to address the situation, getting worked up yourself about how inconsiderate and selfish her husband is, indignant on her behalf.
    - Reset. One way to stay in your lane is to acknowledge that she is part of this dynamic and is making a choice to tolerate it. You do not need to judge her willingness to participate, nor do you need to take it on and get worked up on her account. She's made a choice. You can't want to fix it more than she does. Choose to listen or not. This part is important. You do not have to participate in enabling others to stay stuck. This is where using your words effectively comes into play. Be kind, say the thing she may not like but you feel must be said, then detach from how she chooses to proceed.
- The culture at work around tolerating sub-par performance is driving you insane. You are so tired of seeing people who aren't up to the job being allowed to continue on their path of mediocrity, impeding the progress of those around them or actively disrupting the team dynamic through emotionally unintelligent behavior. There is one such person on your team who is making life harder for everyone else. What do you do? Staying in your lane could look like one or more of the following:
    - Observe and make note of what, specifically, you are witnessing. If you are on the receiving end of such interactions, speak up. Tell the person what you see and how you feel about it. Let your manager or boss know that you had the conversation and what triggered it.

- Keep doing what you need to do. If you are in a position to influence how the situation is handled (e.g. you're a manager or executive), then do it. If people at your level don't speak up in favor of positive change, what will change? Keeping the peace at the expense of all the other dynamics in play isn't a strategy. It's hiding from the tough stuff that needs to be addressed.

As you can see, staying in your lane isn't just about separating yourself from what doesn't concern you. It's also about doing what you are capable of doing and not wussing out of it. This is when who you are as a high achiever can particularly benefit you and others. If your lane is leadership, behave like a leader. If your lane is friendship, be a true friend. If your lane is the path of growth and development, stay the fuck out of situations where you are dissecting the paths of others. We are each on our own journey, and on that journey we have various lanes to navigate. You don't have to master them all at one time, but be willing to examine your behavior in any given situation and determine the path that keeps you moving forward in a way that has the highest interests of all in mind. What is in someone's highest interest does not necessarily equate with what they want. It's often what we don't want and try our best to avoid that is in our best interest to see and confront. I am not suggesting that you strive for perfection here. You can and will at times make the choice or decision that doesn't quite align; you learn from each and every experience. The key is to be conscious and make choices reflective of self- and other-awareness.

Identify the Why

Our emotional reactions to others can lead us astray when we aren't willing to look deeper and examine the motives. When anger was my primary defense mechanism, I sure as shit wasn't staying in my own lane. In fact, I was looking for all possible reasons to direct my attention outward rather than inward. Once I understood that I did so in order to avoid the layer of hurt beneath the anger, it gave me what I needed to check myself. Why did I get so mad when my friend stayed with her alcoholic boyfriend? To me, it was stupid. I couldn't make sense of it, so I would get mad and worry about her and then judge her for not making the decision I would make. I still have friends who make choices that blow my mind. I still get triggered, but now I immediately stop and question myself. Do I want something for them that they aren't willing to move toward yet? Why am I the one who's pissed off when they are the one in the sucky situation? I then determine what the best way to stay in my lane is, whether it's to kindly point out that they have a choice to stay stuck or create something new, or if I've done that too many times to count, I may choose to stay silent and let them have their say before changing the subject. This often leads to a response like, "I know, I know! I should speak up and demand something different, but..." There's no need to add anything. They know, they are making the choice. The end.

So much of what triggered me at work and in my personal life was seeing the unmet potential in others. Why do people insist on repeating their mistakes, making choices that don't move them forward, complaining incessantly as if they are victims in their own lives? It made me positively crazy, this commitment to the crappy status quo, when a tiny amount of energy expended in a different way could make a huge difference in the life of the person in question. I had to freaking get over it. It's not my burden to make sure everyone I come into contact with makes the most of their life. That's their quest. I want to be a part of it when it makes sense and serves both of us, but, when it doesn't, taking it personally that they won't just do the thing already is a total waste of precious energy I could be directing to everything else we've been discussing up to this point.

Work situations in particular can be frustrating beyond belief. As high achievers, we tend to have very specific ideas about the "right" way to do anything. We look at the decision of another, don't get it, ask ourselves "What the fuck?" start cataloging the way we would do it, and basically dive down the rabbit hole of judgment and disapproval. While there are certainly times when a coworker has proven time and again that they aren't up to the task, generally speaking, this isn't the case. If you are in an environment where there are more of those people than the competent, stop reading this immediately, and get right on how you're going to get the eff out of Dodge. Most of the time, the people whose actions you are examining are competent. They may not work as quickly or be as decisive or as efficient as you are, but so what? Are they getting the job done effectively? Why do they need to do it your way? What are the other qualities they possess that are significant, yet eclipsed in your mind by how they operate? Are they steadfast? Calm? Dependable? Does your leadership trust them to get the job done? There is no one way to do something, and your way isn't necessarily better. Maybe you are faster and more efficient. Are you also less tolerant and more irritable? Back off. You aren't the other person. If they are doing their job competently and have gained the trust of those around them, then it's not your place to worry about how they are getting things done. You would want to be trusted to do your job, right? Extend the same courtesy to others. It's the right thing to do to have a conversation when something is negatively impacting the team or you. But if not, and it's a matter of "my way is better," drop it. Your way is just your way. We are all built differently. Appreciate the positives in others and acknowledge their strengths. If you're lucky, you work in an environment where the various strengths of the team members are complementary rather than the same.

To Don't:

- **Don't be nosy.** Whatever it is that's going on with someone, it's none of your business unless they choose to share.
- **Don't pass judgment.** You never, ever have the full picture of the details of someone's life, and it's a convenient distraction that keeps you from looking at your own shit.
- **Don't get caught up in the frustration of what others will or won't do.** People will either meet their potential or they won't. It's not your place to be involved unless they ask for your help.

Do Instead:

- **Treat others as you wish to be treated.** Yep. It's that simple.
- **Examine triggers and determine what they reveal about *you*,** rather than being caught up in the actions of the person who triggered you.
- **Be conscious and intentional about behaving in ways that are aligned to the highest version of your role in a given situation.**

Summing Up

Our modern world makes it nearly impossible to keep our heads focused on our own lives. Not only do we all get exposed to the tribal behavior of grouping up according to our "superior" characteristics, now we have an entire social media industry that enables us all to be in one another's business all the time. It takes discipline to avoid the easy way out of judging the lives of others to direct our energy away from ourselves; we try to escape the difficult emotions that are trying to communicate with us, if we would just take a minute to look inward instead of exploding outward. Indulging in emotions like anger, irritation, and judgment create feedback loops that keep us stuck in a place where we don't grow and can't flourish. It takes deliberate, conscious effort to interrupt our usual way of doing things to establish new, more productive ways to engage with others while in a state of high self-awareness that serves everyone involved.

Start paying attention to how you can be most effective by staying in your lane.

1. Come up with some examples of triggering relationships, personal and professional, where you tend to slip into judging the other. Why are you triggered? Is it because you want something better for them? Do you believe you have a better way of accomplishing a task or goal?
2. What does your reaction, internally and externally, consist of? What you do say outwardly? What do you think internally? Write down your thought process and include the emotional component. For instance, if you have a coworker who does things in a way you find baffling, your thought process may consist of, "I don't understand why he does it that way. It takes too long and it's super irritating."
3. Is there a theme in these scenarios? Are you judging others through the lens of how you would do it? Do you want others to meet their potential and get frustrated when they don't? Are there situations where you could help or have valuable input, but you don't want to rock the boat, so you stay out of it?

4. Once you are clear on the "why" behind the triggers, run the same scenario, or a future potential one, through your head. How will you react differently? What does it look and feel like to stay in your lane in that particular situation? Practice your responses and how you'll change your internal dialogue as well as your external reactions. The goal is to step away from the reactivity, not get worked up over someone else's situation, acknowledge that your way isn't the only way, the person doesn't have to be ready to tackle whatever this is, etc.

Each one of us is on our own journey. Remember that and do your best to be true to yourself and continue heading in the direction you've chosen.

PART IV

Smooth Operator

CHAPTER 12

Show Up and Use Your Words, FFS

For as long as I can remember, I've had a polarizing effect on those I meet. Most people have a fairly strong and immediate reaction to me. It's either, "She tells it like it is—I freaking love it!" or "Oh, that bitch...? I don't think so." There are very few people in the "not sure what to think of her" camp when it comes to me and the opinions I elicit in others. These reactions can be traced back to the single most obvious thing about me in pretty much all situations: I'm a truth-teller. I'm a straight shooter. I communicate concisely, without a lot of extra words that provide comfortable padding or a circuitous route of communication used to deliver underhanded criticism or sneaky truth. I say what I mean, and I mean what I say. Some dig it, others hate it. For me, there is no other way to be. But that doesn't mean it's been easy for me to show up 100 percent myself in all situations; I have had my fair share of struggle with giving this essential part of myself freedom of expression. I've been through periods when I decided to keep my mouth shut in favor of keeping the peace, only to find that the negative impact on me personally made it not worth the effort. Even though I had many past experiences that made it clear this was the case, I was surrounded by so many people who made a habit of staying silent that I was goaded into trying it out from time to time to see if it made life easier in some way. It didn't. It made it worse, and I watched how it made life harder for the person working so painstakingly to make sure everyone else was okay.

Staying silent, censoring yourself, or otherwise hesitating in any way to show up is about putting the comfort of others ahead of your need to express who you are. People-pleasing is among the most pervasive ways in which we put ourselves last on the list of priorities in any given situation. We are raised to be polite, to engage in small talk, avoid uncomfortable topics, make sure the needs of others are met, keep the peace, and the list goes on. When you tie yourself in knots to choose precisely the least triggering words or shut up altogether, you're left feeling depleted, temporarily relieved by the quiet outcome that didn't rock the boat, but continued to widen the black hole inside you, sucking up your energy and the words you really wanted to say but didn't. And how does this behavior actually serve you? You've eaten the words that you should have expressed, and they take up residence inside you, desperately wanting a way out that you won't give them through your voice. They swirl, fester, and lurk, waiting for an opportunity to explode outward when you've finally had enough. Make no mistake—keeping your words inside is harmful. The words represent unexpressed, suppressed emotion. You can only do that for so long before you begin to suffer the consequences. Why wait until the consequences show up?

When you are constantly watching your mouth, the consequence is that others don't actually know who you are. What if you've been triggered by someone's rude behavior but hesitate to respond because you are busy coming up with the politest comeback you can muster? You know why you hesitated, but the other person doesn't. They could interpret your hesitation as weakness or a lack of confidence. And if you're thinking, "Who cares what they think?" Well, the answer is that you do, obviously. There are real consequences to that, especially professionally.

I once worked with a lovely woman who was a lifelong pleaser. She knew it was a problem but was struggling with how to stop worrying so much about what others thought of her words and actions. Early in our work together, she expressed frustration that she would not infrequently get requests to cut her commission. She was irritated and confused by this, because she knew that many of her colleagues were rarely asked to do so. I asked her how else this was showing up for her professionally, and she said she felt that contractors and others involved in her transactions were more frequently disrespectful of her time and expertise than she believed to be the case with others in her position in general. When she told me the story of a disagreement she'd had with a contractor, I asked her what was going through her mind during the interaction. She said she was angry, so it took her a bit of time to come up with her response. To the other person, she appeared to hesitate. I asked her to tell me what she really wanted to say, and I told her those words would have been appropriate. They were not rude, but they were direct. As we continued to talk through it, it became clear that her hesitation tended to show up in situations where she felt she had to justify her position or assert her expert opinion. The hesitation was about her attempt to avoid being seen as arrogant or contrary if her expertise was at odds with the thoughts of the client or contractor. She had even lost the opportunity to work with potential clients from time to time, as this hesitation to speak directly with confidence in her expertise was interpreted to mean she would not be an effective negotiator if it became necessary. While you are not to be overly concerned with what others think, you do need to be mindful of creating a false impression of who you are through incomplete expression. You are here to be you. Will that piss people off? Maybe.

Here's the thing about trying not to trigger others: you cannot control the reaction of the person you are talking to. Tying yourself in knots to avoid doing so is a total waste of your time. The first of three keys to speaking up that I'll share in this chapter is:

Speaking Up Is Not a Creation of Conflict

It is not up to you to make it okay for others. We've been taught to be nice when, quite frankly, being nice is a crock of shit. Nice?? "Nice" is not useful. "Nice" doesn't even have a particularly great connotation. A synonym of nice is "agreeable," and it's the predominant meaning when we engage in people-pleasing. Who said agreeable is desirable? To be agreeable implies malleability. You will make sure to appear agreeable, even if you're not on the inside. The negative impact doesn't end with you, either. How is it good for the person you're engaged with to only hear what they wish to hear? Isn't that something we generally look down upon? My corporate experience was liberally sprinkled with coworkers who delivered watered-down messages to leaders so they would fit the bill of being "nice," "agreeable," and generally relaying information that would be pleasing to hear rather than the truth. How does that policy move anything or anyone forward? You cannot grow or help facilitate the growth of others if you concern yourself with being nice. If you are a person who expects this kind of behavior from those around you, it's time to cut it out. Now. Is your self-esteem so fragile that truthful words from others threaten you in some way? Why? Deep self-examination is necessary if this has been an issue for you. If you don't feel up to doing it on your own, find a therapist or coach to facilitate the process so you can move on with creating the life you are capable of having. This brings us to key point two about speaking up:

Be Kind, Not Nice

Prioritizing kindness means saying what the other person *needs* to hear, not what they *want* to hear. When you first begin making the transition in your communication, you could run into some tricky situations. Remember, you are not here to judge. If your best friend is involved in something you don't agree with, that's okay—your job is not to impose your will on your bestie. Say your piece with compassion and kindness, without trying to make him/her do what *you* think is the right course of action. You can give advice if asked, but keep in mind there is no obligation on their part to take the advice given.

Several years ago, I had a friend—we'll call her Bree—who would constantly flake on plans. She had a lot going on in her life, but the chaos was self-imposed, the result of her unwillingness to speak up for her own needs when it came to her relationship and her professional life. I stopped giving her advice when it became clear that she was deeply entangled in the patterns she had established.

At times, I thought nothing less than a catastrophe would shake her out of her misery. I stayed in my own lane until her behavior began to negatively impact me.

When I was on maternity leave with my second daughter, Bree texted me one day to ask if she could come by to see the baby and bring us a meal that week. I told her she could choose the day that worked best for her. She did but didn't show up. I didn't reach out to her because, by this point, I already knew that there was a 50/50 shot, at best, that she would show up for any given plans laid. She texted me again, not long after that, to once again suggest that she come by to see us. This time, my response was to share how long I would be home on leave and that she could let me know when she wanted to come by. Again, I didn't hear from her. She didn't end up coming by at all during my maternity leave, and she also didn't bring it up the next time I saw her. It was as if none of it had ever happened. I was not okay with it, but again, I didn't bring it up.

Several months later, I included Bree's daughter, Ava, on the invite list for my older daughter's birthday. She responded that they would be there and that Ava was excited to come to the party. I told my daughter Ava would be there, and she was happy she would have the chance to see her. The day of the party, Bree and Ava didn't show up. I checked my texts and emails, but she hadn't sent any messages to say they couldn't make it. I thought perhaps something unexpected had come up so, even though I was irritated, I gave her the benefit of the doubt. After a few days with no word, I decided it was time to say something. I emailed Bree and let her know that her inability to honor plans made me feel as if our friendship wasn't a priority. Her lack of follow-through was disrespectful of me and my time, but not showing up for a birthday party also affected my child and, without any kind of follow-up on Bree's part, I had no answer for why they didn't show. I told her that I was aware of the chaos in her life and had no illusions that I was the only person she did this to regularly. I also said that she might be under the impression that her behavior is acceptable just because no one has said otherwise, and I wanted her to know it wasn't okay with me. What she chose to do with that information was her decision, but I wasn't going to continue to silently participate. She responded very apologetically and told me that she had forgotten about the party when they made a last-minute decision to travel. Bree didn't even register that they had missed it until I brought it up. Our friendship faded away after that. There was no fight, no confrontation beyond the email. I even saw her after that, and our interaction was fine. But I knew that it was highly unlikely she would change her behavior, and I wasn't willing to tolerate it.

Your first reaction may be to cringe, believing that this is the dreaded outcome. True connection involves reciprocation of respect, first and foremost. If you continue to prioritize the needs of others over your own, you continually send yourself a message about your value and how it doesn't measure up to the value of the person or people you put first. You've been so trained to be nice that stating your truth in a calm and collected way makes you uncomfortable, even if it's the other person who has been thoughtless in their approach. They may quickly realize this, apologize, and promise to do better in the future. If so, that's great, but expect the improvement and know what you'll do if you don't see it. If you get a defensive reaction, that's okay, too. They may need time to cool off, but that doesn't mean you shouldn't have said anything. Why should you continue to be frustrated, enabling thoughtless behavior that impacts you negatively? Just to keep the peace? To what end? In cases like this, you should use your words in a way that is authentic to you, but not in a way that prioritizes the needs of the other person over your own. There are a couple of really important reasons for this:

1. How will the other person know that the status quo is unacceptable if you don't speak up?
2. How will the situation improve if you don't give voice to how it's not working for you as it is?

It's easy from where we sit to make all kinds of assumptions about what's going on with someone else, what they should be aware of, when they should be reaching out to you, how you'd like to be treated, but the truth is, sometimes we are too inside our own heads and lives to be as aware as we should be of others and how we are interacting with them. If your friend is surrounded by people that allow him/her to flake habitually, how can you expect him/her to behave differently? From where they sit, it hasn't been an issue. No one has said so, therefore there is no impetus to change. This is exactly why I let Bree know how her behavior impacted me, and brings us to key point three:

Give Others the Opportunity to Respond

Stop assuming you know what the other is thinking, what they'll say, how they'll react to you sharing your thoughts on a particular situation or behavior. You have no idea. Sometimes people will surprise the hell out of you if you'll give them a chance. Sometimes you'll get the response you expected, and the information helps you evaluate your relationship to this person, how/whether it's serving you, and what must take place mutually in order for you to stay engaged. If you're someone who expects people to read your mind, stop. No one can give you what you expect if you don't vocalize it. If you've spoken up and still don't see improvement, it's time to establish your line in the sand. What will you tolerate and what won't you? You get to decide, but spending time feeling hurt, anxious, or pouty, when you haven't said the words or revisited a lack of forward movement, is a waste of energy.

It's equally important that you identify a way to do this in your professional life. It may feel more threatening to you when it comes to your career; it's a perfectly reasonable approach to start with personal scenarios not related to work to begin finding your voice and practicing what feels authentic. There is a possibility you'll be so exhilarated by expressing yourself that you'll take it too far if you're not careful! The same lovely woman who struggled with people-pleasing in the professional scenario had decided to practice using her voice in personal situations. She got such a charge from doing so that she practically floated into one of our sessions, so pleased with her sense of empowerment that she said if she wasn't careful, she would "tell everyone to go to hell!" She was joking, of course, but the new sense of power woke her up to just how much she had suppressed herself to that point, and now it felt like a dam of emotion and empowerment would burst and flood forth, taking out whatever happened to be in its path, if she didn't stay alert and mindful in her communication. Her close friends had noted the change and gave her tons of positive feedback, letting her know that they observed and appreciated this newfound confidence she carried herself with. This is how you know you have the right people around you. They celebrate your growth and transformation.

One day, about halfway through my career, I had an experience that made me pause and question how best to handle subtly inappropriate comments that I could have decided weren't worth confronting. I was discussing an upcoming trip with two women I respect and regard as friends. We chatted with one another individually and were working out the details about which of us should travel when I received an instant message from my executive. The message said: "I hear there's bickering over who should attend the trade show."

Pause.

Bickering?? Oh, hell no. The sexism oozing from this statement was screaming in my face, but I felt certain he had no idea that it came across that way. I also understood it was unlikely he would have used that term had a man been involved in this conversation. I was no delicate flower, wilting in the presence of male authority, accepting of the sexism that was so ingrained in corporate culture. I would never accept it, and I was often the squeaky wheel that pissed everyone off by doing that truth-telling thing when others wouldn't. I had to make a decision in that moment about how to confront the situation, because I knew he was oblivious. I also knew I couldn't let it go. It was a completely inappropriate choice of words, and a totally unnecessary intervention on his part. We had already resolved who would go. There was zero tension in the exchange. It was a factual and practical discussion that had reached a conclusion, yet here he was, interjecting himself.

Him: "I hear there's bickering over who should attend the trade show."

Me: "Bickering? No. There's no bickering. We were discussing it."

Him: "What's the problem?"

Me: "There's no problem, and no bickering. We are adults and had a very reasonable discussion about it. It's been resolved."

Him, sensing my tone: "Oh, okay. Well, that's good."

I didn't scream "SEXIST REMARKS!" at him, but I made it clear by repeating his word choice and how we resolved it that he had chosen poorly. I wanted to make my point without getting into a knock-down drag-out with my executive, and I definitely wasn't willing to ingratiate myself by pretending I needed his help. If we had been talking in person, the discussion would have been more direct. Did it solve the problem from that point forward? It depends on what "solve" means in that context. I wanted him to have awareness, and from that perspective, it did work. He was more respectful (and a bit more careful) with me going forward, but I have no way of knowing if that extended to others, or if he knew who would/wouldn't tolerate it and behaved accordingly. This is where a lot of people get tripped up, thinking that it's not worth speaking up because you can't change the other person. Trying to influence others is the wrong primary goal. The goal is to be true to yourself by speaking up when you are not okay with how something is going down. When you speak up, you do your part to express yourself and make clear what you will not tolerate from others. How the person on the receiving end handles it is up to them. They will either internalize the message specifically or more broadly, e.g. I can't treat Jane that way because she calls me out, versus I can't treat people that way because it's not right. If they don't internalize it at all, then you have another set of decisions to make around how to handle it going forward, whether to involve anyone else in the conversation (especially in the case of work situations) and whether you are going to stick with this person for more of the same. There's no one right answer, but saying nothing is the wrong answer.

I worked with a lot of really great guys during my tenure in corporate. Those I had friendship connections with would privately tell me how much they hated what they witnessed in terms of sexist behavior or exclusion of women from leadership positions in favor of less qualified men just because they were dudes. One friend in particular would make pointed statements at team lunches about how they were engaged in yet another "sausage fest" all-male outing, no women to be found. It always fell on deaf ears, but he didn't stop saying it. But for every guy who was willing to speak up, there were many who observed and said nothing because they were too much a part of it to see the issue, they weren't being targeted specifically, or they figured it would make no difference. In every one of these possible scenarios, who is served by silence? Not a single person. Not those dishing it out, not those taking it, and not those standing on the sidelines saying nothing. No one is served by silence when it comes to seeing and speaking out against any form of behavior that hurts others, whether it's at the one-to-one level or at a group/community level. You cannot assume that oblivious people won't see the light. Maybe they won't, but how does that excuse you from saying what you should? Imagine how many rights we wouldn't have in our society if people didn't stand up and speak out against what is unfair or unjust? We are obviously talking about scale here, and I'm not suggesting you have to run right out and join a march. You can make a difference every day by speaking up at the micro scale, with those who surround you. Dismiss the ridiculous notion that you know the outcome of speaking up. You don't, and going back to the earlier point, you are withholding the opportunity for response from the other when you stay silent.

None of us is in this world alone. You are not here to march to orders and keep your mouth shut. If you don't show up fully, and do so in a way that is visible and audible, you severely limit the kind of life you will live. When you hide behind socialization and fear of conflict, no one can really see you. *You,* who you are at your core. Not everyone will like you, but my gods, if everyone did, what would that say about you? Life is not a popularity contest. People who pursue it as such generally suffer terribly, unhappy in their lack of authenticity and running around like headless chickens making sure everyone else is okay. Think of the people you admire most. Are they people-pleasers? Or do they show up authentically, totally themselves even if others don't like it? You don't have to like everyone, and not everyone has to like you. I prefer to know who people really are. Even if I'm not on the same page with someone in every way and don't want to hang out with them personally, I respect people who show up as themselves, so I know how to work with them effectively if needed. I'd rather know who has the knife out for me than someone who takes it out the minute I turn my back. Would you rather be around those who fake it or those who are honest?

The beautiful side effect of showing up authentically is that you open yourself up to a brand-new world of connections and possibilities. When you are genuine, people can really see you. They will come forward and want to be your friend, business associate, or partner. They respond to your authenticity, and, as cheesy and overplayed as it sounds, you will create your tribe in this way.

To Don't:

- **Don't decide there is no point in speaking up.** The outcome is not the goal. Speaking up *is* the point.
- **Don't put the comfort of others above your own.** Do not tie yourself in knots trying to find a way to keep the peace at your own expense.
- **Don't stay silent because you are worried about how the other person will react.** You can't control the reactions of others; staying silent to avoid reactions is the choice that harms you.

Do Instead:

- **Give others the opportunity to respond.** People may surprise you if you give them a chance instead of projecting their reactions.
- **Be kind, not nice.** Nice is useless. Kindness is about respect. Say the hard things that need to be said out of respect for the person you're saying them to.
- **Detach from the outcome.** It may not go the way you want it to. You still have to use your words.

Summing Up

Forever holding your peace may work for quelling wedding objections, but it's no way to get through life. The use of your voice is critical to showing up authentically. When you fear rocking the boat or creating conflict, decide there's no point, and generally eat your words, the person you hurt the most is you. Shutting up and taking it to make others more comfortable is a recipe for personal disaster. It leads to habitual self-silencing or self-censoring, which creates a pattern of disempowered thinking and behavior that doesn't serve you or the people around you. When you decide not to speak up for fear of creating conflict, you make yourself judge and jury, having decided the outcome in your own mind without allowing the other person the chance to respond. The outcome is not within your control; using your voice to speak up is. The single most important job you have in this lifetime is to SHOW UP. Be you. You're here for a reason. You aren't here to stay at the bottom of your own priority list. Speaking up with authenticity empowers you to be yourself, allows others to see who you really are, and lays the foundation for a life lived on your own terms, rather than catering to the imagined needs of others that you've manufactured inside your own head through your need for control over your interactions.

When you're not accustomed to using your voice, it can be scary to get into the habit. Approach it one step at a time.

1. Consider the situations in which you avoid speaking up now. Who are you are most wary of? What kinds of situations make you really uncomfortable? Are you better at doing it in one area of your life, with certain people, personally or at work? Is this a general issue for you? Do you tend to default to silence when there's an opportunity to speak up?
2. Why do you hesitate? Take full inventory. Are you afraid of the other person's reaction, worried about what they will think of you and what you've expressed, or do you believe that nothing will change, so why bother? Consider as many angles as you can, so you get a clear picture of what contributes to your reticence.

3. Review your notes so far and determine which of these situations feels least threatening to you. What one area can you focus on to address in the next thirty days? What do you want to say? How might you say it? If the thought of it makes you feel like puking, that's okay. Once you have one or two interactions under your belt, that feeling will fade. The muscle of speaking up will get stronger and it will come more easily over time.
4. Create a top three to five list for what you will address over the next thirty days, and come up with your plan for flexing your voice muscles. After the first few, it's highly likely you will naturally start doing it more and won't need to rely on a system of accountability to keep you going. If you do need a little support at first, tell someone you trust what your plan is and set up a time to check in. Chances are you can help this friend out and inspire them to do the same in their own life.

CHAPTER 13

Be Tenacious and Trust

In the lead up to my corporate exit, life inside my head was strange. At times I was nearly euphoric, floating dreamily along, barely grounded in the reality that I was actually going to do it, leave the relative comfort and safety of a job that compensated me well and provided a fairly cushy material lifestyle. Inevitably, my euphoria would wane, leaving space for the doubts to creep in. The self-questioning kicked in, my ego incredulous that I was crazy enough to contemplate leaving with little idea of how I was going to make it all work. Don't get me wrong—I had a plan, of course, but everything included in my plan was foreign to me. I'd never had to market myself to make a living before, not in the way I knew I had to going forward. I had done my research and had an intellectual grasp of the tasks and activities I would tackle, but the only evidence I had that it would work came from others. I didn't have any first-hand experience to rely upon. I was about to embark on a massively high-stakes experiment with no knowledge of the outcome. While that made it an exciting prospect, it also stirred up nearly equal parts of fear and holy-shit-ness inside me. Why did I think I could pull this off? The stats are pretty bleak when it comes to entrepreneurial success rates, with some research showing as high as 90 percent of endeavors fail within five years. I could have taken one look at that number and run screaming back in the direction of comfort and safety, but I didn't. Cars aren't the safest things to drive around in either, but I don't avoid driving my car because it could be dangerous, and neither do you.

When it comes to changing your life, you must be tenacious in the pursuit of what you envision. Bring your high-achieving A game and make it happen. If you don't bring it and your tenacity, it won't work. Period, end of story. You might as well stay put. Whether it's starting your own business or creating a life that works for you inside an existing corporate structure, you will face your own demons many times over. You must be prepared, with mental padding and helmets, to take yourself on. You are your own worst enemy when it comes to transformation. You are the one who has to overcome your programming through consistent effort so that you're ready to commit like crazy to what it is you want instead. Now, more than ever, is when you need the people with fierce belief in you to be by your side. They can't fight the battle for you, but they are like armored reinforcements, ready to kick you back into the arena when you try to leave, because they know, even when you waver, that you are meant for this. They know how bad you want it and how hard you've worked for it, and they will not allow you to give up on yourself. Your commitment to yourself has to be the biggest and baddest it's ever been, and for this reason you are in truly uncharted territory. You've likely never been your own champion in the way that you must be now. And your commitment to being the champion of your own cause will be tested.

Early in 2016, I started to seriously contemplate my future. I didn't know what I wanted at that point, so I started carrying a notebook everywhere and jotting down my thoughts compulsively throughout the day. The glimmer of a different life began to form. Every day, I looked forward to writing down my evolving thoughts and the inspiration that was coming in. As is often the case when you begin to forge a new path, opportunities started to show up. Most of the time, they weren't the right ones. But once in a while, an opportunity that did make use of a natural ability of mine would pop up, and for a time I would have shiny object syndrome. I would think "YES! I can totally do this, it's easy, I already know how," etc. Usually, it was something that kept me playing small. After a time, I would come to the conclusion that it wasn't the right thing and go back to focusing on my big, much scarier, vision until the next shiny, less scary object came along. That all stopped that summer, when I got a wake-up call in the form of a weather event.

One hot July afternoon, my family and I were indoors. My husband and children were in the basement playing and hanging out. I was on the second level of our home, two floors away. I worked out that morning and had just showered. Through the large window in our master bathroom, I noticed that the light outside had changed and that the sky, sunny not long before, was overcast. I love overcast skies and adore summer storms, so I perkily anticipated a good one must be on its way. As I was drying my hair, I saw a blinding flash of blue light and heard an explosion, nearly simultaneously. Every fire alarm in our home immediately began blaring. I dropped the hair dryer and ran to the top of the stairs, calling down to see if my family was okay. Luckily, they were. My husband and I started looking around outside our home (after we waited a while!) to see where the lightning had struck, as that was the only explanation that made sense, even though no rain or storm had followed the strike. I had seen the flash of light from our bathroom, so we looked in that area behind our house and didn't see any evidence of a strike. As we walked around upstairs, we found the evidence in our daughter's room. An outlet had been pulverized by the heat, blown off the wall, and turned to ash. There were black streaks imprinted on the wall above the outlet. The lightning had struck our home, snaking its way around the tree in front of the house to hit right below the roof line by our daughter's bedroom. Once I knew our home had been hit and not some nearby tree, I had a shaky moment of realization that I had been holding a hair dryer when it occurred.

The lightning strike did some damage, taking out multiple electronics and requiring us to rewire our home. Strangely, with no evidence to suggest it, I felt that the strike was some kind of message to me that I needed to focus on the big things I had been dreaming about. I was still screwing around at that point, torn between this or that idea, still wandering toward what felt safer. It seemed like the embedded message was that I would be safe to pursue the big scary thing. After all, I'd been using a hair dryer when my house was struck by lightning and was unharmed. When I look back, I realize that moment marked a turning point for me.

I stopped chasing the comfortable and committed to doing the big thing. It took months to get back into a normal flow at home, with safe wiring and replacement of damaged electronics, but it was barely a blip on the radar. No real harm had been done, and I had been jolted (ha!) out of my wishy-washy mental meandering.

I had additional tests of commitment once I'd already decided to leave. In the last few months of my career, it was like every element that had been out of alignment for me was suddenly magnified. The team I had worked so hard to build was taken away from me. I was given a new set of teams, all of which needed some serious TLC on both the personnel and strategic fronts. I had proven that I could effectively manage teams in that state, so my "reward" was to give the healthier team that had been my responsibility to someone I saw as less competent and to give me more issues to manage. This came right after I had been informed my promotion had been blocked by one of the most toxic executives I'd ever had the misfortune to work with. Whatever irritations, annoyances, situations, or people I no longer wanted to tolerate that had fed into my decision to leave were in my face. I was beyond frustrated at that point and would sometimes mutter crazily to myself and to whatever forces were at play, "I'm already leaving, gah! I know! I'm not planning to change my mind, so knock it off." It was as if an invisible hand was at my back, firmly pushing me toward the exit, making life extra uncomfortable, a continuous reminder of why I wanted to leave and to continue right out the door. As painful as it was, I also appreciated the reminders. I knew they were meant to be reinforcements of my decision to leave, and they definitely had that effect. If any doubts remained, the last stretch before my final exit erased them.

When you embark on the quest to transform your life, expect the shit to fly. It will, because even when you don't quite grasp how, the tests are for your benefit. It's as if the entire infrastructure of your life must be upgraded, and the tests that come in find the weaknesses that must be addressed. Having doubts? A test will find them. Have inadequately supportive relationships? A test will show you. Committed as fuck to getting what you know you deserve? A test will ensure you're serious. It's not comfortable. It's not supposed to be. Have you ever read or seen a hero movie where the hero didn't start by overcoming some serious bullshit? People don't find their inner strength through ease. They must be tested, so that what isn't as strong as it should be becomes stronger, and anything that may impede progress can exit. When tests show up, be grateful. It means you're on the right path, that there's something worth testing you over. If the path you're on isn't quite right, pay attention. The tests that show up might be just what you need to correct course.

Trust the Process

If there's one thing we human beings really suck at, it's staying the course when we aren't flooded with overwhelming evidence that a decision we've made is totally 100 percent spot-on the most right thing ever. Our ability to have the patience to allow events to unfold has been beaten out of us, replaced with a bludgeon-like approach in which we continue to hammer and push and fret over why something isn't going the way we thought it would, desperately searching for "the answer" that will allow all to fall into place, and quickly at that. For high achievers especially, the attachment to the hustle-and-grind way of life provides the false sense of control we cling to so we can force things to go our way if it becomes necessary. None of that is going to work for you going forward. Now that you're convinced you must trust yourself above all, it's time to learn how to trust the process overall.

Oh, I struggled mightily with trust at the beginning of my journey. I would make a move or decision and then wait impatiently for a sign or response that meant I had made the right move. The urge to fix, adjust, or amend my actions in some way would come on strong, and I'd have to proverbially sit on my hands and remind myself to give it time. Because I had spent so much effort on personal development, I had the false sense that any move I made had to be the single step that would get me from point A to point B. I would think, man, I really thought that through, why didn't it go as I expected? And that right there, the curiosity and openness to the answer, was the first step toward establishing trust in the process. You must accept that there is a degree of uncertainty in this quest.

You will not have all the answers or know what the outcome of a given decision or endeavor will be. It's when you insist on having that information that you participate in your own stagnation. You don't have to race for the finish line. You do have to take the next inspired step in a process and wait for the next inspired step to show up. I refer to this uncertain state as the haze. It's as if there's a veil of fog between you and where you're going. It's not nowhere; you know there is something beyond the haze, even if you don't know what it is yet. And honestly, isn't it a little exciting to watch life unfold before you? Do not insist that unknown = bad. Find a spirit of adventure and excitement, and expect the best for a change. There is a freedom that comes with finding trust in the unfolding. When you expect the best, you can approach the uncertainty as if it's a lovely surprise that will be revealed to you when it's time.

I've been in this place many times over the last couple of years. I had a dream that has stuck with me since I had it, its symbolism so meaningful and beautiful that I can instantly conjure the visuals of the dream and the feelings that came with it. In this dream, I was on a flat barge, riding over a river. There was someone behind me, using an oar to steer us through the water. The water was a bit rough, and because there were no sides on this vessel, I was looking down, keeping my balance, and watching the water. When we came close to land, I had to take a big step from the barge to the shore. Once I was on solid ground, I breathed a sigh of relief and looked up, astonished and in awe of what I saw. I was on a beautiful beach, and there were huge, shiny, beautiful buildings on the horizon. This place was beyond my expectations. I knew I had been on a journey to somewhere, but I hadn't anticipated the destination would be as grand as it was.

The meaning of this for me was clear. I was and am focused on taking the steps and being on the journey. The person behind me, ensuring that we stayed afloat and pointed in the right direction, represented the Process. I trusted this entity to steer, and I focused on what I needed to do, which was to stay on the vessel and take the step between it and the shore when we arrived. The scene on the beach represents the outcome, and even though I still don't know what it is, I know it's beyond my ability to comprehend right now. This was such a clear message to me that it had the effect of cementing my belief that all is well and will be well, if I'll only do my part and trust the rest will fall into place. I don't have to know what comes next.

Opening to Opportunity

One of my favorite questions these days is when someone asks, "Where do you see yourself in five years?" My answer is "I don't know, but I can't wait to see what life is like!" Of course, I have intentions for how I want my life to be in terms of how I feel, how I spend my time, where I want to go, and what I want to experience. But the truth is, professionally, I don't know. I couldn't have predicted, when I left my corporate job, that I would be doing what I'm doing now. I was still thinking fairly small at that point, in terms of establishing my business, attracting clients, showing up on social media, etc. Those things all still matter, but I hadn't anticipated speaking, leading retreats, and writing a book. What comes next will be linked to all these activities, but in ways that I can't yet predict. I have been delighted by the kinds of opportunities that have come my way, and sometimes awe-inspired by how timely and significant certain meetings with new people have turned out to be.

This may sound like some mystical bullshit to you, but I'm telling you, there's no harm in trying this approach. You have nothing to lose and everything to gain. No matter what your religious or spiritual beliefs are, there are certain laws at work in this world that are inexplicable. Despite my training in genetics, or maybe because of it, I know not everything can be explained. But you can open your mind, try it, and observe what happens next. I have friends who are hard-core skeptics in this regard, who've told me excitedly that opportunities started coming their way after they articulated an intention to do something differently. That's just how it works. Not every opportunity that comes up is the right one; this is a refining process. It's incredibly rare for people who've had to overcome enormous amounts of programming to know what comes next for them, right out of the gate. You will go through a period of contemplation, and opportunities will arrive in order to assist you. The opportunities that come in provide just enough detail and include enough of what you think you may want that you actually consider it. During this consideration process, you will identify what you like about a given opportunity and what isn't quite the right fit. You can move forward with that additional information, with further refinement to your own want/don't want list, and keep going.

You will continue to have these opportunities to refine until you have the certainty you need to either instantly recognize the aligned opportunity when it shows up, or to create your ideal professional scenario given what you've learned. Here are some examples of how this has played out for a few of my clients and friends.

- Jessica, a highly talented producer, has been considering starting her own business for years. She's not quite ready to make that decision, so part of her exploration is contemplating the possibility of taking on a business development role with a particular type of organization. Within weeks of saying the words out loud, that type of organization reached out to her regarding an opportunity to do business development. She was able to see the details associated with the role and concluded that, though the role sounded good, she wasn't sure the organization was the right fit. She moved on, excited that not only had something quickly materialized for her consideration, but she could move forward with more information about what she wants through having evaluated the option.
- Casey is a well-respected leader in the non-profit world. She is one of the first names that come to mind for organizations seeking fresh leadership. Fundraising and working with numbers are particular strengths of hers, which opens up possibilities well beyond the world she's been in for so long. Her family depends on her salary, so money is a non-negotiable consideration with any potential opportunity. After a session in which we sat down to talk through how she wanted to feel professionally, what kind of work energizes her, etc., she received an unexpected call to consider a role in real estate, operationally managing a large office with the potential to grow beyond that. The money was fantastic, and she had the skills to do the role effectively. After several conversations with those trying to recruit her, she concluded

that it was too much of a departure from what truly inspires her, and that it wasn't worth making the move based on the money opportunity. Very importantly, she prioritized how she wanted to feel and what she had defined as the most inspired parts of her work to date over a financial decision that could have lured her in.

- Elizabeth is in a solid senior management position and enjoys her job but knows there's something more for her. One of her recent projects was to oversee a financial software implementation, and she was completely energized by the work. As a process-oriented person, it had all the right elements to hold her interest, and she began to wonder if she had a future in software consulting. Not much later, she was approached by just such an organization about a job opportunity. As was the case in Casey's scenario, the money was great, but it required more travel than she wanted and didn't align with her intentions regarding her family and time with them. She passed but knows that there could be other such opportunities in the future that will be a better global fit for her.

This truly is the fun part! Look forward to it. Be open. During this time, people may ask you to do something you hadn't considered, and, at times, you may wonder if you have what it takes to do what's been asked of you. This is when trusting the process requires you to take a giant leap of faith. You must tune in to the signs and messages that come to you in various forms during this time. Again, whether you believe in any of this or not, give it a try and see what happens. Your openness and willingness to suspend disbelief can serve you in ways you can't imagine. If you're not a believer now, you'll be converted. It's practically a guarantee.

When an expected opportunity or a request that you do something you've not done comes in, pay attention, especially if the same type of opportunity comes up repeatedly. I knew that I would someday hold retreats as part of my business. It didn't feel like a near-term consideration, so it was one of those ideas I had jotted down in my notebook and held onto for the future. After a period in which I had several speaking engagements and met new people through a couple of my good friends (themselves highly successful in business), I was asked three times in the span of one week if I could facilitate retreats. Two of these opportunities were for corporate groups, one was for an offsite retreat that would serve those who are ready for transformation but unsure of how to get started. Suddenly, my future retreat thoughts became present-day considerations. Was it a little scary to think about? You bet. But I was being shown that others trusted me to do this effectively for the people they had in mind. I couldn't let the fact that the timeline was different stop me from moving ahead. I had to acknowledge that, like many other things I'd been shown should happen sooner rather than later, I'd still feel some fear and wonder if I could pull it off, no matter the timeline. The only thing putting it off did was postpone the experience of working through that part internally.

There's no going around the personal development and stretching that trusting the process will require of you. You have to go through it. You can decide when to go through it, but when an exciting opportunity shows up in a strong way for your consideration, don't dismiss it as a fluke. It may be that now *is* the time. Accept the fear and self-doubt as part of the process and move forward with courage.

Watch for Signs

Pay attention to signs and messages and accept throughout this process that they may range from very subtle to not-so-subtle. Most signs are fairly subtle until you learn to recognize them, then you can't help but see them frequently and when you need them most. For me personally, music has always been a major source of confirmation of my path or decisions, in particular the titles of songs. This has been true for years and years, but my attention to this particular message modality rose to new heights after a particular experience that really showed me the power of this sign. After I had my first child, I went through a period of pregnancy loss followed by infertility. It was devastating, as anyone who has experienced loss and infertility can attest to. I had started to wonder if I would be able to have another child. I had never taken pregnancy for granted—after all, as a genetic counselor, I knew everything that could and did go wrong for others—but I had assumed, after having a first healthy child, that I would be able to have another. After a time, it became clear that something physical might be wrong and I decided to seek the help of a specialist. Around that same time, the song "I Will Wait" by Mumford & Sons would come on, frequently when I was wondering about my chances of having another baby. More times than I care to admit, it made me burst into tears. Over the course of a couple of years, it became my beacon. I knew I would have another child, I just didn't know when. I found out that I needed surgery to correct a physical issue, and fortunately, it was a simple outpatient procedure. After I had recovered sufficiently, we were given the green light to try to conceive again. The week I planned to take a pregnancy test, "I Will Wait" came on the satellite radio station nearly every time I was in the car. It was then that I knew I was pregnant, and that the test would confirm it. And that's exactly what happened. Years later, when I was in my contemplative mode regarding my future, songs such as "Ready to Start," "Let It Happen," and "Something to Believe In" would come on right when I was in mid-thought about a move or path I should consider. Strange, right? I can't explain it, but I don't need to. It's become integral to trusting my process.

Signs have shown up for me in so many ways when I've needed them the most, and they show up for you, too. Learn to recognize them by paying attention to the following:

- Music, like my example. It can be in the title, the lyrics, the song may be attached to a memory or a particular person or loved one. You can interpret its meaning from your perspective.
- Actual signs, like billboards, bumper stickers, license plates, in the form of ads or images online, etc.
- Numbers. You may see the same time on the clock repeatedly or see certain numbers displayed over and over again. You can look up the number(s) to learn what they mean. You may be surprised at the robustness of numerology and what it can tell you.

- Words that come from those around you, whether they are near and dear to you or strangers. People will often say something you need to hear right when you need to hear it. Pay attention!
- Animals might make some interesting appearances. The belief in animals as messengers is an ancient one, and much like numerology, there is a ton of information out there for the curious. If nothing else, have some fun with it. I'm willing to bet you will be shocked when you see that the blue jay that's randomly been showing up in your tree has a meaning that aligns with just where you are in that moment.

Signs and messages can provide the added support you need to stay tenaciously committed to your path when tests show up. Remember, even if you don't believe in any of it, there's no harm in tuning in to what's happening around you that can be supportive to what you are creating. Furthermore, you don't have to actually do anything except pay attention. If it doesn't work for you, cool. If it does, you'll love having that mysterious layer of support to help keep you going.

To Don't:

- **Don't give up.** No one said this would be easy.
- **Don't keep yourself small.** If it doesn't make you feel a little like throwing up, your vision isn't big enough.
- **Don't fold when you're tested.** You will be.

Do Instead:

- **Pay attention to the signs and messages** that show up to support you. It's some of the coolest and most fun reinforcement you'll experience.
- **Trust. The. Process.** Follow the breadcrumbs that show up, and trust they will when it's time.
- **Expect the best. Suspend disbelief. Be tenacious.**

Summing Up

The transformative journey requires a huge commitment on your part. You have to experience the vision you've created for yourself so completely in your heart and mind that making it to that place is the only option. This is the quest of your lifetime, but you'll also never be done. Everything you learn to do here you will have to repeat over your lifetime, unless you suddenly decide you've had enough growth and expansion for one lifetime, thank you very much, which is highly unlikely when you experience the benefits of having stuck it out through fear, uncertainty, letting go of control, speaking your truth, showing up as yourself—the list goes on. And the more you repeat the steps in the process, the more second nature they become. Will it be hard the first time? Yep, without a doubt. Mostly because you've never done it before, and anything new takes more effort the first time. If you are willing to do the deep work that at times feels hard but is also totally exhilarating, then you will transform yourself and your life. You will be empowered in a way you've never been before, and you'll see the people around you in a new and empowering way. Life itself will be a completely different experience when you approach it from a place of courageous authenticity. You will be unstoppable.

The following will help you become accustomed to taking a trusting approach with yourself and the world around you.

1. There's no instant gratification. Don't try to fast-forward through the process! The journey is a critically important learning experience that reinforces your faith and trust so that you may go forward and repeat the process as often as you choose to.
2. Weather the tests. You will be challenged; expect and embrace it. The challenges have the power to refine and redouble your commitment. They are tests of your faith in yourself, how badly you want the vision you are working toward, and whether you will stay committed to yourself throughout, not allowing the bumps in the road to throw you off-track entirely.

3. Adjust your vision if needed. In case you haven't noticed, rigidity has no place on your quest. Be flexible, adapt as you learn, and change your vision or tweak it as necessary. The process requires the ability to be agile and open.
4. Find your center. Remind yourself of why you began this journey and how it's already positively impacting your life. Your choices are to keep going for something better or resign yourself to what you wanted to leave behind to begin with. When the going is a little rough, reach out to your supporters and cheerleaders, or your pals who are on a similar journey, and support one another.
5. Remember that people or situations may exit your life during this time to make room for new ones that are better aligned to you and where you're headed.
6. Above all, STAY PRESENT. It's when we dwell on past outcomes or predict doom and gloom in the future that we falter. Look out your window and appreciate what you see, give thanks for the cup of coffee in your hand, for your health or your home, the chair you're sitting in—it really doesn't matter. Gratitude, even for the smallest things, takes you out of the energy of fear and doubt. It's the single easiest and most powerful way to shift yourself out of a dark spiral and back to reality.

Trust yourself. Trust the process. Enjoy the quest.

CHAPTER 14

Who Cares, Anyway?

After an entire book's worth of information regarding how it's all about you, I'd like to remind you that it's not all about you. We live in a world filled with people we barely take the time to consider or see when we are steeped in our own problems and misery. Unhappy people are self-focused by necessity. When you're unfulfilled, your energy is spent on figuring out how to get out of that place to a better one. You get through daily life with an underlying energy of duty and obligation, typically to everyone but yourself, and fall into bed at the end of the night, drained, because you haven't actually seen to your own needs in the endless, repetitive cycle. When you're in a place of survival, you focus on yourself. You don't have the bandwidth to think of others. It was this realization about myself that galvanized me into action. I wanted to contribute, to know that I could take action that would benefit people beyond just me and my family, and in doing so could set an example for my children and hopefully inspire others to do the same.

Successful, high-achieving people have the advantage of material comfort and often have means far beyond what they need to survive. Unfortunately, the material comfort often comes at a personal price that is depleting in all the ways we've discussed up to this point. When you commit to bettering your life, to thrive instead of just survive, you have the energy to contribute to others. It's not just a nice place to be, it's what you should strive for. The world is a beautiful, heartbreaking place filled with need. As human beings, we are accountable for the world we live in. If we don't see it that way, what's the point of life? We take action in large and small ways all the time to make the world a better place. We may give a couple of bucks to the man at the intersection begging for money, hold the door for an elderly person, give an encouraging smile to a kid who looks worried about climbing the jungle gym, donate toys and clothes for the holidays, etc. These are all worthy ways to show up, and we should keep showing kindness to others above all. But when you have more means than most people, how can you take it to the next level? How can giving be something that's a part of your default mode of operation all the time, rather than something we are reminded of only during the holidays or when we are asked to pay attention?

If there's something you're passionate about, seek out opportunities to participate in some way. There are so many great causes in the world that it can be overwhelming to try to choose which to pay attention to. Don't worry—there are plenty of interested people for any given cause. Look for what really lights you up and find a way to participate. For me personally, injustice in any form is intolerable to me. There are a ton of causes that tie to that theme, so I've made a point of looking into opportunities that are particularly significant to the cause of justice. It's my personal mission to give of my time and resources to people who are systemically held back due to race and socioeconomic status in order to help them break that cycle for their own children and future generations. Government has a role to play, but the inequality in the system will not be addressed until enough squeaky wheels get together to bring attention and action to the situation. I, for one, aim to be a squeaky wheel and help those impacted by the status quo.

What pulls at your heart? What need do you see that makes you wish you could do more? There's always something you can do. Figure out what works best for you and do it. Make it a part of your mission on earth to make life a little better for others. Collectively, we have power beyond what we can imagine. Be a part of the collective power and encourage your like-minded friends and family to do the same. You can even find something mutually significant and work together to make a positive impact. Imagine how powerful it would be if you recruited just one person, who recruits another and so forth... That's the kind of power that can have real impact in our world.

You may know people who are involved in the pain of others to the exclusion of themselves. You know, the person who lives and breathes protesting, giving, and putting the needs of the needy above their own to the point where they may be living on the couch in their parents' basement. That is not the kind of contribution we are talking about here. The person who focuses exclusively externally is out of balance and has made a habit of being depleted. Not you, though. You have the insight and wisdom to know that your own tank must be full in order to give most effectively. Taking the time to eat right, exercise, sleep, spa, golf, vacation, and live to your fullest potential is what will keep your tank full so you can keep going and giving.

Here is a final To Don't list to take with you into your transformation.

To Don't:

- **Don't stay stuck.**
- **Don't keep grinding it out.**
- **Don't accept less than you deserve.**

Do Instead:

- **Commit to living up to your potential.**
- **Believe in yourself and the world that surrounds you.**
- **Make progress and let go of perfection.**

Your life is meant to be an experience. Make it a joyful one, and do what you can to help make it better for others. I know you can do it. You're a high achiever, after all.

Acknowledgments

Thank you to everyone who helped me co-create my dream of publishing this book. I am so grateful to be surrounded by family, friends, and supporters who have shown unwavering faith in me, even as I faced fear and self-doubt. I couldn't have done this without the unconditional love and support of my husband Payam and our little girls, Syra and Sansa. Thanks to Lee Constantine, for being a disrupter in the publishing industry and providing a platform, Publishizer, to aspiring writers while offering his wisdom and knowledge throughout the process. Through that platform, I connected with Brenda Knight and Mango, the ideal editor and publisher to help me share my message. Thank you for taking a chance on me. A special thank you to everyone who supported this effort by pre-ordering the book, especially those who went all out and ordered a bunch at a time as a show of their faith in me: Kristin Malfer, Angie Salmon, Charity Ohlund, Dick Flanigan, Jacqui Chapman, Courtney Thomas, Adriana Bates, Blake Nelson, Jessica Hao, Katie Grimes, Mike Miles, Stephanie Culver, and Nancy Whitworth. Thanks to Sarrah Chapman, my soul sister, for being by my side throughout this process, and to my other besties Sarah Ruppert and Emily Fish, for their belief in me.

Acknowledgments

Resources

Below is a list of the books and other resources that were of pivotal importance to my self-development journey. This is not all-inclusive, but these are the favorites that I suggest you check out to support you on your quest.

Books

The Big Leap: Conquer Your Hidden Fear and Take Life to the Next Level by Gay Hendricks

This excellent book will prompt you to think about whether you are meeting your full potential or staying in a safe but successful zone of operation. Gay Hendricks shares stories of super high achievers who truly appeared to have it all yet remained unfulfilled until they took a, well, big leap, into their zone of genius where all the magic awaited them. He talks about how to make that leap by forming new and better habits and thought processes to unleash your potential.

The Desire Map: A Guide to Creating Goals with Soul by Danielle Laporte

The title of the book says it all. This was the first book I picked up when I started to wonder what the hell I was chasing and why whatever it was eluded me. Danielle challenges you to rethink the way you set goals, stop chasing the thing you've set your sights on, and start considering how the heck you want to feel when you reach the goal. I credit this book with getting me to be specific about my current and desired emotional state. Words matter, especially when you use them to sketch the vision of your future.

The Science of Getting Rich by Wallace Wattles

This is a seriously old-school book (published in 1910!) with a highly relevant message about how your thoughts and beliefs about money can enhance or hinder your ability to make it. Wallace describes thinking in The Certain Way, that is, the money-making way, and what it takes to transform your beliefs in this regard. It is essentially a lesson in the Law of Attraction that applies beyond money to all areas of life. If you get a kick out of old books, this one is for you.

The War of Art: Winning the Inner Creative Battle by Steven Pressfield

Whether you're a creative type or not, Stephen delivers a compelling message about overcoming blocks in order to take your art, project, business, or craft to the next level. His focus is on overcoming Resistance (fear), and he uses historical and cultural data to drive home the impact of fear on all areas of life, along with a strategy for addressing it. Stephen also provides the tools to create the mental toughness and discipline required to see whatever it is you're working on to completion.

You Are a Badass: How to Stop Doubting Your Greatness and Start Living an Awesome Life by Jen Sincero

The highly entertaining Jen delivers her self-help message through funny personal anecdotes, colorful language, and gentle encouragement in *You Are a Badass*. She helps you identify limiting beliefs and behaviors so you can create a life you love. Jen's own experience is as a struggling-turned-successful writer, but the messages and lessons resonate whether you are a creative type or not. Above all, she wants you to love yourself.

Other Resources

Along with reading, I did a lot of listening on my quest to fulfillment. Here are the two standouts that I highly recommend.

Podcast: *The School of Greatness* with Lewis Howes

Lewis's story is truly inspiring. His promising athletic career was cut short when he sustained an injury, leaving him jobless, aimless, and living on his sister's couch. He began the journey to find his purpose and has since become a bestselling author and motivational speaker. His podcast features his own story, as well as interviews with other inspirational people who have forged their own paths to their greatness. I listened to this daily to pump me up on walks around the corporate campus. I highly recommend you listen, especially if you prefer audio to reading.

Firestarter Sessions by Danielle Laporte

These sessions were an audio series that has since been compiled into an audiobook. The sessions are closely aligned with the message in *The Desire Map*, detailed above, but with the added power of hearing the conviction in her voice as she convinces you to focus on your strengths, forget about balance, and get the clarity you need to kick some ass at life.

About the Author

Maki Moussavi is a corporate career veteran and Master's trained genetic counselor who left the glory of societally defined success to become a transformational coach, motivational speaker, and author. Over the last several years, she has focused on personal development and how to help high achievers create fundamental change in the pursuit of fulfillment.

Maki has a passion for helping people see their true potential and supporting their journeys to raising the bar for their lives. Her ability to break down complex concepts into accessible and actionable information was the backbone of her corporate achievements and is a critical component of her coaching and thought leadership.

Her background as a clinician who pursued a corporate career established a diverse skillset with expertise in communication, presenting, sales, and management. Through speaking, coaching, and writing, Maki leverages the process she has created to jumpstart rapid and lasting transformation in the executives and high achievers she works with, using the wisdom and knowledge gained through her education and her own journey from being stuck to being aligned.

Find more content at www.makimoussavi.com.